Reissued 11/5/78.

FILE COPY
PROPERTY OF: ASSOCIATED BOOK PUBLISHERS

WITHDRAWN

D1429378

UP THE LINE TO DEATH

Also edited by Brian Gardner

THE TERRIBLE RAIN
The War Poets 1939–1945

UP THE LINE TO DEATH

THE WAR POETS 1914-1918

AN ANTHOLOGY

selected and arranged, with

an introduction and notes by

BRIAN GARDNER

FOREWORD BY EDMUND BLUNDEN

EYRE METHUEN

11 NEW FETTER LANE · LONDON EC4P 4EE

First published 1964
by Methuen & Company Ltd
Second edition published 1978
by Eyre Methuen Ltd
This anthology © 1964, 1978 by Brian Gardner
Printed in Great Britain by
Redwood Burn Limited
Trowbridge & Esher

ISBN 0 413 45580 7

Above all I am not concerned with Poetry.
My subject is War, and the pity of War.
The Poetry is in the pity.

WILFRED OWEN

FOREWORD

I remember a cheerful soldier from the East End of London, a private, in the spring of the year 1916, 'somewhere in France'. The place where I particularly see him is a 'saphead' or advanced position in the British front line, where he and another were having a quiet afternoon after a hideous and killing night. He was sitting on an ammunition box when on my trench round I looked in and had his welcome. But I was interrupting him. He was composing a poem! He at once asked me to read it, and some others, all addressed to his wife. I fear that he was never again to see her in this life.

Up to the year 1916 that Western Front, so far as the 'British Expeditionary Force' was in occupation, was the home of many young poets. A subaltern in my battalion, killed in the Second World War, wrote charming humane verses, which he set no value on. For myself, I could show my attempts to my commanding officer, to the brigade major, even to the brigadier-general, without shyness. Indeed General Hornby *ordered* me to place my Ypres pieces before him, even at the beginning of the year 1917.

There were still in Ypres at that date poets who kept something of the idealism of 1914 in their outlook and their poems. But that was the Passchendaele year, and to me it seems that the Passchendaele 'drive' was murder – not only to the troops but to their singing faiths and hopes. From then on the voice of those who found strength and interval enough merely for penning their visions was generally a cry. Some, of course, right from the start, had now and then foretold and expressed 'the image and horror of it', amid their affectionate evocations of their suddenly distant loves.

I have not before me as I write A. G. Macdonnell's wonderful book *England, Their England*, but he more or less said what I am trying to say by way of prologue to the present anthology; it was not after all a nation of shopkeepers but of poets. That gentleness which is the base and force of good literature had come home to me from many experiences before August 4, 1914, and insisted until all was over; although I will admit that poetry is not invariably triumphant. An anecdote: early in 1919, at a dull village near historic Valenciennes, my new colonel at breakfast told me to give a lecture on poetry to the battalion. I draw a veil over that. At least all officers and other ranks stayed to the finish, and it was a freezing morning in an immense German wooden hall.

In the very next village, but I did not know, there was a young and gallant officer named Edgell Rickword. Some years later I came upon the few war poems that he has published, and it is true to say still, 'I remember'.

It is a singular thing for one who passed through the valley of the shadows so long ago to be returning to it, fifty years afterwards, and yet it is a great moment when these survivors discover good companions in the new generation; their compassion, their imaginative sympathy, their enquiring spirit make up for a multitude of sins and forgettings. Of this new generation Brian Gardner is a representative. He has his world as in his time, but he longs to do homage to those who looked beyond death, or who were horrified by schematic death into a new poetry, half a century since. His anthology of the Brooke, Sassoon, Owen generation, though one or two earlier books of the sort are not yet dead asleep on our shelves, is not only a literary achievement of the first order, but a testimony of the spirit of man worthy of the 'lost generation'.

EDMUND BLUNDEN

CONTENTS

To Unknown Lands

CONTENTS

Home Front

Death's Kingdom

A Bitter Taste

Behind the Lines

O Jesus, Make it Stop

At Last, at Last!

ACKNOWLEDGEMENTS

Thanks and acknowledgements are due to the following who have kindly allowed us to use poems: Messrs George Allen & Unwin Ltd for poems by Richard Aldington from *Collected Poems 1915–23*; Messrs A. D. Peters for a poem by Martin Armstrong from *The Buzzards and Other Poems* (Messrs Secker & Warburg Ltd); the Author's Representatives and Messrs Sidgwick & Jackson Ltd for poems by Herbert Asquith from *Poems 1912–1933* and *The Volunteer and Other Poems*; the Literary Executrix and Messrs William Heinemann Ltd for a poem by Maurice Baring from *Collected Poems*; Leonard Barnes and Messrs Peter Davies Ltd for a poem from *Youth at Arms*; The Society of Authors as the literary representative of the Estate of the late Laurence Binyon for poems from *The Four Years* (Messrs Macmillan & Co. Ltd); Charles Scribner's Sons for a poem by John Peale Bishop from *Now With His Love*, copyright 1933 Charles Scribner's Sons, renewal copyright © 1961; Messrs A. D. Peters for poems by Edmund Blunden from *Undertones of War* (Oxford University Press); the Author's Representatives and Messrs Sidgwick & Jackson Ltd for poems by Rupert Brooke from *Collected Poems*; Harcourt, Brace & World Inc. for poems by e. e. cummings from *Poems 1923–1954*; copyright 1923, 1951 by e. e. cummings; the Author's Representatives and Messrs Sidgwick & Jackson Ltd for a poem by Jeffery Day from *Poems and Rhymes*; Messrs William Heinemann Ltd for a poem by Geoffrey Dearmer from *Poems*; the Author's Representatives and Messrs Sidgwick & Jackson Ltd for a poem by John Drinkwater from *Collected Poems*; Messrs Putnam & Co. Ltd for a poem by Lord Dunsany from *Fifty Poems*; Messrs John Murray (Publishers) Ltd for a poem by J. Griffyth Fairfax from *Mesopotamia*; Mrs Frankau for a poem by Gilbert Frankau from *The Judgement of Valhalla* (Messrs Chatto & Windus Ltd);

Messrs A. D. Peters for a poem by John Freeman from *Collected Poems* (Messrs Macmillan & Co. Ltd); the Author's Representative and Messrs Macmillan & Co. Ltd for poems by Wilfrid Gibson from *Collected Poems 1905–1925*; International Authors N.V. for poems by Robert Graves from *Fairies and Fusiliers* and *Poems 1914–26* (Messrs William Heinemann Ltd); Messrs Burns & Oates Ltd for a poem by Julian Grenfell from *Julian Grenfell*; Wyn Griffith for a poem from *The Song is Theirs* (Penwork, Cardiff); the Trustees of the Thomas Hardy Estate and Messrs Macmillan & Co. Ltd for poems from *Collected Poems*; the Author's Representatives and Messrs Sidgwick & Jackson Ltd for a poem by F. W. Harvey from *Gloucestershire Friends*; Sir Alan Herbert and the Proprietors of *Punch* for a poem from *Half-Hours at Helles* (Messrs Basil Blackwell & Mott Ltd) and a poem from *The Bomber Gypsy* (Messrs Methuen & Co. Ltd); Sir Alan Herbert and Messrs Methuen & Co. Ltd for a poem from *The Bomber Gypsy*; Messrs John Murray (Publishers) Ltd for poems by W. N. Hodgson from *Verse and Prose in Peace and War*; the Society of Authors as the Literary Representative of the Estate of the late A. E. Housman and Messrs Jonathan Cape Ltd for a poem from *Collected Poems*; the *New Statesman* for a poem by Philip Johnstone reprinted from the *Nation* of 16 February 1918; Messrs Faber & Faber Ltd for a poem by David Jones from *In Parenthesis*: Mrs Kettle for a poem by T. M. Kettle from *Poems and Parodies* (Messrs Gerald Duckworth & Co. Ltd); Mrs George Bambridge and the Macmillan Company of Canada Ltd for poems by Rudyard Kipling from *The Years Between* (Messrs Methuen & Co. Ltd); Messrs Herbert Jenkins Ltd for a poem by Francis Ledwidge from *Last Songs*; Messrs Constable & Co. Ltd for a poem by P. H. B. Lyon from *Turn Fortune*; Messrs Constable & Co. Ltd for a poem by D. S. MacColl from *Bull and Other War Verses*; the Proprietors of *Punch* for a poem by John McCrae; Messrs Herbert Jenkins Ltd for a poem from *Soldier Songs* by Patrick MacGill; *The Observer* for a poem by R. B. Marriott-Watson; Messrs Curtis Brown Ltd for a poem by A. A. Milne from *The Sunny Side* (Messrs Methuen & Co. Ltd); Mrs Monro for a poem by Harold Monro from *Collected Poems* (Cobden-Sanderson); Captain Newbolt for a poem by Sir Henry Newbolt from *Poems New and Old* (Messrs John Murray (Publishers) Ltd); Literary Executor of Estate of Robert Nichols for poems from *Invocations* and *Ardours and Endurances* (Messrs Chatto & Windus Ltd); Messrs Chatto & Windus Ltd for poems by Wilfred Owen from *Poems*; Lord Selborne for a poem by Robert Palmer from *The Life of Robert Palmer* (Messrs Hodder & Stoughton Ltd); Mrs Dorothy Plowman for poems by Max Plowman from *A Lap Full of Seed* (Messrs Basil Blackwell & Mott Ltd) and *Shoots in the Stubble* (Messrs Daniel Ltd); Messrs Faber & Faber Ltd for poems by Herbert Read from *Poems 1914–34* and *Collected Poems*; Edgell Rickword for a poem from *Behind the Eyes*; Messrs Chatto & Windus Ltd for poems by Isaac Rosenberg from *Poems*; Siegfried Sassoon for poems from *Collected Poems 1908–1956* (Messrs Faber & Faber Ltd); R. H. Sauter for a poem from *Songs in Captivity* (Messrs William Heinemann Ltd); Messrs Constable & Co. Ltd for poems by Alan Seeger from *Poems*; Messrs Ernest Benn Ltd for a poem by Robert Service from *Collected Verse*; Mrs Shanks and Messrs Macmillan & Co. Ltd for poems by Edward Shanks from *Poems 1912–32*; Messrs David Higham Associates Ltd for a poem by Osbert Sitwell from *The Selected Satires and Poems* (Messrs Gerald Duckworth & Co. Ltd); Messrs Gerald Duckworth & Co. Ltd for poems by Osbert Sitwell from *Selected Poems Old and New*; Cambridge University Press for poems by C. H. Sorley from *Marlborough and Other Poems*; Messrs John Murray (Publishers) Ltd for a poem by Edward de Stein from *Picardy and Other Poems*; Lord Glenconner for poems by E. W. Tennant from *Worple Flit and Other Poems* (Messrs Basil Blackwell & Mott Ltd); Mrs Helen Thomas and Messrs Faber & Faber Ltd for poems by Edward Thomas from *Collected Poems*; Messrs Ernest Benn Ltd for a poem by Edward Thompson from *Collected Poems*; Oxford University Press for a poem by W. J. Turner from *Selected Poems 1913–36*; Messrs Hope Leresche & Steele for a poem by R. E. Vernède from *War Poems* (Messrs William Heinemann Ltd);

Messrs A. D. Peters for a poem by Alec Waugh from *Resentment* (Messrs Grant Richards); Willoughby Weaving for a poem from *The Star Fields and Other Poems* (Messrs Basil Blackwell & Mott Ltd); Messrs Methuen & Co. Ltd for a poem by I. A. Williams from *New Poems*; Mrs W. B. Yeats and Messrs Macmillan & Co. Ltd for a poem by W. B. Yeats from *Collected Poems*; the Author's Representatives and Messrs Sidgwick & Jackson Ltd for a poem by E. Hilton Young from *Verses*; Messrs David Higham Associates Ltd for poems by Francis Brett Young from *Poems 1916–18* (Messrs William Collins Sons & Co. Ltd).

We should also like to make acknowledgements to the following for permission to use songs: Messrs Francis, Day & Hunter Ltd for the chorus of 'Where Are the Lads of the Village Tonight'; Messrs B. Feldman & Co. Ltd for the chorus of 'Take Me Back to Dear Old Blighty'; Messrs Chappell & Co. Ltd for an extract from a song by Paul A. Rubens, 'Your King and Country Need You'.

Every effort has been made to trace executors, but in some cases they could not be found. The editor wishes to apologize for any omissions due to this in the 'Acknowledgements'.

INTRODUCTORY NOTE

This book is intended as a tribute to those who fought, and died, in the First World War. There have been many accounts of that unparalleled tragedy, and here is yet another: one written by the men who lived through it.

Those who wish to ponder, with or without prejudice, on tactics and strategy, or to know How It Happened, must turn to other volumes. This account has nothing to do with that: it is traced on the emotions of men at war. Each poem has been selected because it tells part of the whole story.

A large proportion of the poets here represented died in battle nearly fifty years ago; but not all of them died, and some are most happily very much with us. To the surviving poets of the war, I can only convey my gratitude for allowing me to cross their great and precious past, and ask them to forgive me my trespass.

Some war poems of 1914–18 are very well-known indeed; but others, such as those by E. A. Mackintosh, Robert Nichols and C. H. Sorley, are in danger of being relegated to dusty shelves and, together with whizz-bangs, puttees and wire-cutters, to the memories of aging men. The experiences, and thus many of the emotions, of the poets were no different from those of the rest of their generation; as young officers they were efficient, and by all accounts many were outstanding. The idea – spread about by those who even at this safe distance seem unable to accept the horrors and several disasters of that war – that the accounts of the poets had no relevance to anyone's experiences but their own, is unconvincing; the lice, cold, hunger, fear, wet, and misery were the same.

After July, 1916, the poets differed only in that they were more articulate than their comrades.

It might be thought that no one could have illusions, any more, as to the nature of that war; but this is evidently not so. In 1961 an historian actually compared the casualties at the Battle of the Somme (a matter of 'brave and desperate nations fighting it out man to man') to those at Waterloo. Wilfred Owen, when invalided home, carried about with him a collection of horror photographs of mutilated men at the Front, which he would pull out of his pocket and without a word thrust before verbal warriors who had not been in the fighting.

The poets of 1914–18 found nobility of man in their war, even if they did not find much nobility in war itself. They found a fellowship as exclusive, perhaps, as any there has been in our history: a brotherhood that transcended the barriers of class, strong at the time; of religion, of race, of every facet of society. This was not just to do with regimental pride, although that was part of it. It was the brotherhood of 'Those who were there' – on the Western Front. Those who had not been there were presumed to be incapable of understanding what the experience had been like, and what it had meant. Since 1918 these ties have been among the strongest undercurrents of British life, ranging from British Legion clubs to the corridors of Westminster. Robert Graves's 'Two Fusiliers' is one of the few poems about this bond. It hardly attempts to explain, because the legend is that those who are already of it, know it, and those who are outside, could never know it. Undoubtedly, this must be right, although it does not diminish one's urge to understand.

Edmund Blunden has written: 'The term war poets is rather convenient than accurate.' Many kinds of poet are in this book: Georgians, Imagists, writers of blank verse, classical and modest rhymsters. All this has not been my concern. In general, however, there are, no doubt, two kinds of poem: those that transcend the trenches and barbed wire, and that are great poetry in any company; and those that are, I hope, valid in the context of the war. Which are which is a matter for critical opinion. It is, of course, widely accepted that the poetry of Edmund Blunden, Wilfred Owen, and Siegfried Sassoon is of the first kind. For the rest, the opinion of the critics seems to have varied widely. Isaac Rosenberg has many admirers. Robert Nichols, his contemporary, was not one of them.

On the other hand, Charles Sorley is not generally held in high opinion today, but John Masefield told Nichols that Sorley was potentially the greatest poet lost in the war, and that had he lived he might have become our greatest dramatist since Shakespeare.

Had he lived . . . Charles Sorley would now have been the same age as Robert Graves. Would he have had a comparable reputation? Had Graves not survived, and he very nearly did not, would he have had the minor reputation now of a Charles Sorley, on the strength of one slim volume of poetry? How would the Fabian Rupert Brooke, who would be younger than Siegfried Sassoon, have reacted to the 1930s? What kind of work would he have produced? Would Wilfred Owen, a year younger than Sir Osbert Sitwell, have been a senior man of letters today? Would H. H. Munro ('Saki') have written the great novel of the war, as many believed at the time he would? The answer lies with him in a filled-in shell crater in the Somme valley. The quest is fruitless. Some who seemed to promise great things, and who survived, have never written a line of poetry since. One became a famous educationalist; another a business tycoon. One of the most famous at the time disappeared into Fleet Street and has been there ever since; another took up politics, and became a Cabinet Minister. But who can say for sure whether the talent of an E. A. Mackintosh – hardly out of school – might have developed into a major one?

When the war began most of these poets knew each other, and today the few survivors are nearly all friends. They mostly, at some time or other, enjoyed the encouragement of Edward Marsh or Harold Monro, and, happily, many young writers of the day benefited from the grant awarded Marsh as the great-grand-son of Spencer Perceval, the assassinated Prime Minister. Through Marsh, Winston Churchill also helped some of the younger poets.

Most of the younger men were influenced by Rupert Brooke's fervent patriotism and mystique of Youth. Men like W. N. Hodgson – who were apart at that time from the feelings of the mass of volunteers who had enlisted for various reasons, many of them fine ones, but not in a search for death – followed Brooke headlong to their deaths, for which they seemed almost anxious. They were conscious of belonging to what they believed was a generation of exceptional brilliance, and they may well have been right; they wanted to prove their worth in some really dramatic way. Even Owen, at the time, felt a sense of 'new crusades and modern knight-liness'. It is difficult to over-estimate the influence of Brooke; to his contemporaries he seemed to express perfectly the idealism of 1914. (It is interesting to recall that after the war some of the surviving poets – Gibson and others – benefited in one way or another from the royalties and estate of Rupert Brooke, the man who had sent so many to death with noble and inspiring emotions in their hearts.)

After the Somme it was never the same again. The heroic days were gone. The disillusion, already under way in the work of Siegfried Sassoon and Isaac Rosenberg, came out in an angry flood; but the loyalties, the pull of the Front, had taken on the grip that was never to let go. Even though he was completely disillusioned with the war, Owen returned to the trenches to rejoin the brother-hood; the hell of home, where no one understood, was worse. Siegfried Sassoon, tutoring Owen and influencing the already embittered Osbert Sitwell and others, took Rupert Brooke's place after the massacre on the Somme. His influence can even be seen on a writer as apart from the British poets as William Faulkner.* Siegfried Sassoon believed that the war was being deliberately prolonged by those who had the power to end it. Not only his views, but his robust, factual style, so different from that of the early Georgians, had its influence.

The reason that such a tragically high proportion of the war poets were killed is, of course, that they were mostly junior officers. Most poetry of the time came from the middle and upper classes; working-class writers like Rosenberg were very much the exception. The military caste system was much in evidence; leaders were naturally found among the better-educated, although most of these

* See 'Victory' in *The Collected Stories*, William Faulkner (Chatto & Windus, 1951).

young boys knew nothing of life except the family, school mores, and the battlefield. (The marching songs, however, were in a sense the instinctive poetry of the troops themselves.) The life-expectancy of a young officer was about nine months – or one summer's 'push'. Few of their verses had the benefit of considered rumination until the exact word fitted the mood. The poet might be blown into the unknown before he even had time to scribble down the ideas and words racing in his head. Many of the poems in this book were jotted on to the backs of envelopes and messages, or sent home in letters. Many enjoyed no revision; some were found after death among personal papers and in battle-dress pockets. All the war poets knew, as Julian Grenfell wrote, that every line had to be good, despite the lack of time and application necessary to make inspiration good poetry, as it might be their last.

As Lord Wavell pointed out in *Other Men's Flowers*, before the First World War battle poems were seldom written by men who had been in battle. There were certain things to write poetry about: love, beauty, heroes, nature, life and death. To write a poem about a wagon-wheel crunching over a dead man's face, as Rosenberg did, was something new – too new for W. B. Yeats. It was not that there had not been horrors in war before; it was that, with only a few exceptions, poets had not been caught up in them.

There have been at least three previous anthologies, *Valour and Vision** by Jacqueline Trotter, *War Poetry*† by Robert Nichols, and *Soldier Poets*.‡ Poets in the first were predominantly those who had not been at the Front; there were fourteen poets in the second.

Here, too, is included the work of some poets not actually at the Front. At the start of the war it was the established poets who wrote so many of the stirring, war-like verses. Men like Sir Henry Newbolt and Herbert Trench were not backward in supplying the trumpet-calls to arms. If such poetry seems somewhat out of place now, it did not do so then, and there is little reason why – in the

---

* Martin Hopkinson, 1920; enlarged, 1923.
† Nicholson & Watson, 1943.
‡ Erskine Macdonald, 1916 and 1917.

particular age – it should have done. Some critics, indeed, believe that John Freeman wrote his best poetry at this time. Later in the war, Laurence Binyon, who was deeply moved by the sacrifice of his juniors, wrote what are considered some of his best poems. It would be difficult to find a better short poem from John Drinkwater than his 'Nineteen-fifteen'. Drinkwater, Lascelles Abercrombie and Richard Church were different in their relation to the war from the other poets at home; it was their contemporaries who were being decimated. They wrote a number of sympathetic war poems. Yeats, who was more moved by events in Ireland than by the war, himself wrote one of the most famous of all the war poems; he found inspiration in his doomed Irish airman.* Of all the poets well-established by 1914, the one for whom the war poets themselves probably had least sympathy was Rudyard Kipling; it seems that most of them admired John Masefield more than anyone else. In fact, no one was closer to them than Kipling, who, at first, wrote war poems about the sea and sailors; but after the death of his only son at Loos, his poems and epigrams turned to bitterness, and at times to cold anger. He wrote with the voice of ordinary people: fearing for their sons, indignant at the faceless men who seemed responsible for some trick that no one quite understood, tired and bewildered by the inability of politicians and generals to conclude the war.

Not all the well-known war poems are here. I should like to have included Robert Bridges' 'Wake Up, England' but his publishers and Lord Bridges believe that the author wished this rousing poem, so redolent of the mood of 1914, suppressed. Worse still has been the enforced omission of John Masefield's powerful and important 'August, 1914', for which Dr Masefield would not give permission. Brooke's 'The Soldier' is familiar. Wilfred Owen's 'Insensibility', Robert Graves's '1915', Maurice Baring's 'In Memoriam A.H.', Laurence Binyon's 'For the Fallen' and 'Ypres', James Elroy Flecker's 'The Dying Patriot', Rudyard Kipling's 'For All We

---

* See his Introduction to *The Oxford Book of Modern Verse* (Oxford University Press, 1936, reissued, 1952). Yeats had a 'distaste' for the war poets; Wilfred Owen was not included in his collection.

Have and Are', Richard Church's 'Mud', and Edmund Blunden's 'Another Journey From Béthune to Cuinchy', have all made way for lesser-known pieces, in order to make the collection a publishing proposition. The result may be some unevenness in quality – certainly Leslie Coulson, for instance, was no Blunden – but theme and interest are, I hope, strengthened. Like all anthologies, in fact, this book omits more than it contains. Lesser-known poems for which I was particularly sorry not to have found room were: 'Death in France' by Carroll Carstairs, 'The Beach Road by the Wood' by Geoffrey Howard, 'After Loos' by Patrick MacGill, and 'Private Claye' by D. C. McE. Osborne.

I would like to express my gratitude to Siegfried Sassoon and Edmund Blunden for their generosity, and encouragement, in this project. My thanks also go to John D. Cullen for accepting a shabby typescript, and to Miss A. Macfadyen for copyright research.

The journey from Laurence Binyon's 'The Fourth of August' to Philip Johnstone's 'High Wood' was a long and terrible one; a journey paved with the corpses of a generation. It is a journey which I have tried to trace in this collection; a collection that is, therefore, presented not only as an anthology, but as a book – with a beginning, a middle, and an end. A book written by men who either witnessed or took part in that journey: a book about war.

B. G.

Prelude

Channel Firing

That night your great guns, unawares,
Shook all our coffins as we lay,
And broke the chancel window-squares,
We thought it was the Judgement-day

And sat upright. While drearisome
Arose the howl of wakened hounds:
The mouse let fall the altar-crumb,
The worms drew back into the mounds,

The glebe cow drooled. Till God called, 'No;
It's gunnery practice out at sea
Just as before you went below;
The world is as it used to be:

'All nations striving strong to make
Red war yet redder. Mad as hatters
They do no more for Christés sake
Than you who are helpless in such matters.

'That this is not the judgement-hour
For some of them's a blessed thing,
For if it were they'd have to scour
Hell's floor for so much threatening . . .

'Ha, ha. It will be warmer when
I blow the trumpet (if indeed
I ever do; for you are men,
And rest eternal sorely need) '

So down we lay again. 'I wonder,
Will the world ever saner be',
Said one, 'than when He sent us under
In our indifferent century!'

And many a skeleton shook his head.
'Instead of preaching forty year',
My neighbour Parson Thirdly said,
'I wish I had stuck to pipes and beer.'

Again the guns disturbed the hour,
Roaring their readiness to avenge,
So far inland as Stourton Tower,
And Camelot, and starlit Stonehenge.

THOMAS HARDY
April, 1914

Happy is England Now

*

Oh, we don't want to lose you
But we think you ought to go . . .

SONG

From *The Fourth of August*

Now in thy splendour go before us,
Spirit of England, ardent-eyed,
Enkindle this dear earth that bore us,
In the hour of peril purified.

The cares we hugged drop out of vision,
Our hearts with deeper thoughts dilate.
We step from days of sour division
Into the grandeur of our fate.

LAURENCE BINYON

From *Men Who March Away*

In our heart of hearts believing
   Victory crowns the just,
   And that braggarts must
   Surely bite the dust,
Press we to the field ungrieving,
In our heart of hearts believing
   Victory crowns the just.

Hence the faith and fire within us
   Men who march away
   Ere the barn-cocks say
   Night is growing gray,
Leaving all that here can win us;
Hence the faith and fire within us
   Men who march away.

THOMAS HARDY
September, 1914

Happy is England Now

There is not anything more wonderful
Than a great people moving towards the deep
Of an unguessed and unfeared future; nor
Is aught so dear of all held dear before
As the new passion stirring in their veins
When the destroying dragon wakes from sleep.

Happy is England now, as never yet!
And though the sorrows of the slow days fret
Her faithfullest children, grief itself is proud.
Ev'n the warm beauty of this spring and summer
That turns to bitterness turns then to gladness
Since for this England the beloved ones died.

Happy is England in the brave that die
For wrongs not hers and wrongs so sternly hers;
Happy in those that give, give, and endure
The pain that never the new years may cure;
Happy in all her dark woods, green fields, towns,
Her hills and rivers and her chafing sea.

Whate'er was dear before is dearer now.
There's not a bird singing upon this bough
But sings the sweeter in our English ears:
There's not a nobleness of heart, hand, brain,
But shines the purer; happiest is England now
In those that fight, and watch with pride and tears.

JOHN FREEMAN

1914

The Call

Ah! we have dwelt in Arcady long time
   With sun and youth eternal round our ways
And in the magic of that golden clime
   We loved the pageant of the passing days.

The wonderful white dawns of frost and flame
   In winter, and the swift sun's upward leap;
Or summer's stealthy wakening that came
   Soft as a whisper on the lips of sleep.

And there were woodland hollows of green lawn,
   Where boys with windy hair and wine wet lips
Danced on the sun-splashed grass; and hills of dawn
   That looked out seaward to the distant ships.

In infinite still night the moon swam low
   And saffron in a silver dusted sky;
Beauty and sorrow hand in hand with slow
   Soft wings and soundless passage wandered by.

And white roads vanishing beneath the sky
   Called for our feet, and there were countless things
That we must see and do, while blood was high
   And time still hovered on reluctant wings.

And these were good; yet in our hearts we knew
   These were not all, – that still through toil and pains
Deeds of a purer lustre given to few,
   Made for the perfect glory that remains.

And when the summons in our ears was shrill
Unshaken in our trust we rose, and then
Flung but a backward glance, and care-free still
Went strongly forth to do the work of men.

W. N. HODGSON

England to Her Sons

Sons of mine, I hear you thrilling
To the trumpet call of war;
Gird ye then, I give you freely
As I gave your sires before,
All the noblest of the children I in love and anguish bore.

Free in service, wise in justice,
Fearing but dishonour's breath;
Steeled to suffer uncomplaining
Loss and failure, pain and death;
Strong in faith that sees the issue and in hope that triumpheth.

Go, and may the God of battles
You in His good guidance keep:
And if He in wisdom giveth
Unto His beloved sleep,
I accept it nothing asking, save a little space to weep.

W. N. HODGSON
August, 1914

Peace

Now, God be thanked Who has matched us with His hour,
And caught our youth, and wakened us from sleeping,
With hand made sure, clear eye, and sharpened power,
To turn, as swimmers into cleanness leaping,

Glad from a world grown old and cold and weary,
  Leave the sick hearts that honour could not move,
And half-men, and their dirty songs and dreary,
  And all the little emptiness of love!

Oh! we, who have known shame, we have found release there,
  Where there's no ill, no grief, but sleep has mending,
    Naught broken save this body, lost but breath;
Nothing to shake the laughing heart's long peace there
  But only agony, and that has ending;
    And the worst friend and enemy is but Death.

RUPERT BROOKE

1914

Field Manoeuvres

*

Goodbye-ee, goodbye-ee,
Wipe the tear, baby dear, from your eye-ee;
Though it's hard to part I know,
I'll be tickled to death to go,
Don't cry-ee, don't cry-ee . . .
Goodbye-ee.

SONG

Field Manoeuvres

The long autumn grass under my body
Soaks my clothes with its dew;
Where my knees press into the ground
I can feel the damp earth.

In my nostrils is the smell of the crushed grass,
Wet pine-cones and bark.

Through the great bronze pine trunks
Glitters a silver segment of road.
Interminable squadrons of silver and blue horses
Pace in long ranks the blank fields of heaven.

There is no sound;
The wind hisses gently through the pine needles;
The flutter of a finch's wings about my head
Is like distant thunder,
And the shrill cry of a mosquito
Sounds loud and close.

I am 'to fire at the enemy column
After it has passed' –
But my obsolete rifle, loaded with 'blank',
Lies untouched before me,
My spirit follows after the gliding clouds,
And my lips murmur of the mother of beauty
Standing breast-high, in golden broom
Among the blue pine-woods!

                              RICHARD ALDINGTON

Going in to Dinner

Beat the knife on the plate and the fork on the can,
For we're going in to dinner, so make all the noise you can,
Up and down the officer wanders, looking blue,
Sing a song to cheer him up, he wants his dinner too.

March into the village-school, make the tables rattle
Like a dozen dam' machine-guns in the bloody-battle,
Use your forks for drumsticks, use your plates for drums,
Make a most infernal clatter, here the dinner comes!

EDWARD SHANKS

The Old Soldiers

We come from dock and shipyard, we come from car and train,
We come from foreign countries to slope our arms again,
And, forming fours by numbers or turning to the right,
We're learning all our drill again and 'tis a pretty sight.

Our names are all unspoken, our regiments forgotten,
For some of us were pretty bad and some of us were rotten;
And some will misremember what once they learnt with pain
And hit a bloody sergeant and go to clink again.

EDWARD SHANKS

Drilling in Russell Square

The withered leaves that drift in Russell Square
Will turn to mud and dust and moulder there
And we shall moulder in the plains of France
Before these leaves have ceased from their last dance.

The hot sun triumphs through the fading trees,
The fading houses keep away the breeze
And the autumnal warmth strange dreams doth breed
As right and left the faltering columns lead.
Squad, 'shun! Form fours . . . And once the France we knew
Was a warm distant place with sun shot through,
A happy land of gracious palaces,
And Paris! Paris! Where twice green the trees
Do twice salute the all delightful year!
(Though the sun lives, the trees are dying here.)
And Germany we thought a singing place,
Where in the hamlets dwelt a simple race,
Where th' untaught villager would still compose
Delicious things upon a girl or rose.
Well, I suppose all I shall see of France
Will be most clouded by an Uhlan's lance,
Red fields from cover glimpsed be all I see
Of innocent, singing, peasant Germany.

Form-four-rs! Form two deep! We wheel and pair
And still the brown leaves drift in Russell Square.

EDWARD SHANKS

Death's Men

Under a grey October sky
    The little squads that drill
Click arms and legs mechanically,
    Emptied of ragged will!

Of ragged will that frets the sky
    From crags jut ragged pines,
A wayward immortality,
    That flies from Death's trim lines.

The men of death stand trim and neat,
　　Their faces stiff as stone,
Click, clack, go four and twenty feet
　　From twelve machines of bone.

'Click, clack, left, right, form fours, incline',
　　The jack-box sergeant cries;
For twelve erect and wooden dolls
　　One clockwork doll replies.

And twelve souls wander 'mid still clouds
　　In a land of snow-drooped trees,
Faint, foaming streams fall in grey hills
　　Like beards on old men's knees.

Old men, old hills, old kings their beards
　　Cold stone-grey still cascades
Hung high above this shuddering earth
　　Where the red blood sinks and fades.

Then the quietness of all ancient things,
　　Their round and full repose
As balm upon twelve wandering souls
　　Down from the grey sky flows.

The rooks from out the tall gaunt trees
　　In shrieking circles pass;
Click, clack, click, clack, go Death's trim men
　　Across the Autumn grass.

W. J. TURNER

Officers' Mess

I

I search the room with all my mind,
Peering among those eyes;
For I am feverish to find
A brain with which my brain may talk,
Not that I think myself too wise,
But that I'm lonely, and I walk
Round the large place and wonder – No:
There's nobody, I fear,
Lonely as I, and here.

How they hate me. I'm a fool.
I can't play Bridge; I'm bad at Pool;
I cannot drone a comic song;
I can't talk Shop; I can't use Slang;
My jokes are bad, my stories long;
My voice will falter, break or hang,
Not blurt the sour sarcastic word,
And so my swearing sounds absurd.

II

But came the talk: I found
Three or four others for an argument.
I forced their pace. They shifted their dull ground,
And went
Sprawling about the passages of Thought.
We tugged each other's words until they tore.
They asked me my philosophy: I brought
Bits of it forth and laid them on the floor.

They laughed, and so I kicked the bits about,
Then put them in my pocket one by one,
I, sorry I had brought them out,
They, grateful for the fun.

And when these words had thus been sent
Jerking about, like beetles round a wall,
Then one by one to dismal sleep we went:
There was no happiness at all
In that short hopeless argument
Through yawns and on the way to bed
Among men waiting to be dead.

HAROLD MONRO

No One Cares Less Than I

'No one cares less than I,
Nobody knows but God,
Whether I am destined to lie
Under a foreign clod,'
Were the words I made to the bugle call in the morning.

But laughing, storming, scorning,
Only the bugles know
What the bugles say in the morning,
And they do not care, when they blow
The call that I heard and made words to early this morning.

EDWARD THOMAS

Tipperary Days

*

Where are the lads of the village tonight?
Where are the nuts we knew?
In Piccadilly – in Leicester Square?
No, not there. No, not there.
They're taking a trip on the continon',
With their rifles and their bayonets bright,
Facing danger gladly, where they're needed badly
– That's where they are tonight.

SONG

Tipperary Days

Oh, weren't they the fine boys! You never saw the beat of them,
Singing altogether with their throats bronze-bare;
Fighting-fit and mirth-mad, music in the feet of them,
Swinging on to glory and the wrath out there.
Laughing by and chaffing by, frolic in the smiles of them,
On the road, the white road, all the afternoon;
Strangers in a strange land, miles and miles and miles of them,
Battle-bound and heart-high, and singing this tune:

> *It's a long way to Tipperary,*
> *It's a long way to go;*
> *It's a long way to Tipperary,*
> *And the sweetest girl I know.*
> *Goodbye, Piccadilly,*
> *Farewell, Leicester Square:*
> *It's a long, long way to Tipperary,*
> *But my heart's right there.*

Come Yvonne and Juliette! Come Mimi and cheer for them!
Throw them flowers and kisses as they pass you by.
Aren't they the lovely lads! Haven't you a tear for them,
Going out so gallantly to dare and die?
What is it they're singing so? Some high hymn of Motherland?
Some immortal chanson of their Faith and King?
Marseillaise or Brabançon, anthem of that other land,
Dears, let us remember it, that song they sing:

> *C'est un chemin long 'to Tepararee',*
> *C'est un chemin long, c'est vrai;*
> *C'est un chemin long 'to Tepararee',*
> *Et la belle fille qu'je connais;*

Bonjour, Peekadeely!
Au revoir, Lestaire Squaire!
C'est un chemin long 'to Tepararee',
Mais mon coeur 'ees ʒaire'.

The gallant old 'Contemptibles'! There isn't much remains of them,
So full of fun and fitness, and a-singing in their pride;
For some are cold as clabber and the corby picks the brains of them,
And some are back in Blighty, and a-wishing they had died.
Ah me! It seems but yesterday, that great, glad sight of them,
Swinging on to battle as the sky grew black and black;
Yet oh, their glee and glory, and the great, grim fight of them! –
Just whistle Tipperary and it all comes back:

It's a long way to Tipperary
(Which means 'ome anywhere);
It's a long way to Tipperary
(And the things wot make you care).
Goodbye, Piccadilly,
('Ow I 'opes my folks is well);
It's a long, long way to Tipperary –
('R! Aint war just 'ell?)

ROBERT SERVICE

From an *Untitled Poem*

Light-lipped and singing press we hard
Over old earth which now is worn,
Triumphant, buffetted and scarred,
By billows howled at, tempest-torn,
Toward blue horizons far away
(Which do not give the rest we need,
But some long strife, more than this play,

Some task that will be stern indeed) –
We ever new, we ever young,
We happy creatures of a day!
What will the gods say, seeing us strung
As nobly and as taut as they?

C. H. SORLEY

Untitled

All the hills and vales along
Earth is bursting into song,
And the singers are the chaps
Who are going to die perhaps.
O sing, marching men,
Till the valleys ring again.
Give your gladness to earth's keeping,
So be glad, when you are sleeping.

Cast away regret and rue,
Think what you are marching to,
Little give, great pass.
Jesus Christ and Barabbas
Were found the same day.
This died, that, went his way.
So sing with joyful breath.
For why, you are going to death.
Teeming earth will surely store
All the gladness that you pour.

Earth that never doubts nor fears
Earth that knows of death, not tears,
Earth that bore with joyful ease
Hemlock for Socrates,

Earth that blossomed and was glad
'Neath the cross that Christ had,
Shall rejoice and blossom too
When the bullet reaches you.
> Wherefore, men marching
> On the road to death, sing!
> Pour gladness on earth's head,
> So be merry, so be dead.

From the hills and valleys earth
Shouts back the sound of mirth,
Tramp of feet and lilt of song
Ringing all the road along.
All the music of their going,
Ringing swinging glad song-throwing,
Earth will echo still, when foot
Lies numb and voice mute.
> On marching men, on
> To the gates of death with song.
> Sow your gladness for earth's reaping,
> So you may be glad though sleeping.
> Strew your gladness on earth's bed,
> So be merry, so be dead.

C. H. SORLEY

Magpies in Picardy

The magpies in Picardy
Are more than I can tell.
They flicker down the dusty roads
And cast a magic spell
On the men who march through Picardy,
Through Picardy to hell.

(The blackbird flies with panic,
The swallow goes with light,
The finches move like ladies,
The owl floats by at night;
But the great and flashing magpie
He flies as artists might.)

A magpie in Picardy
Told me secret things –
Of the music in white feathers,
And the sunlight that sings
And dances in deep shadows –
He told me with his wings.

(The hawk is cruel and rigid,
He watches from a height;
The rook is slow and sombre,
The robin loves to fight;
But the great and flashing magpie
He flies as lovers might.)

He told me that in Picardy,
An age ago or more,
While all his fathers still were eggs,
These dusty highways bore
Brown, singing soldiers marching out
Through Picardy to war.

He said that still through chaos
Works on the ancient plan,
And two things have altered not
Since first the world began –
The beauty of the wild green earth
And the bravery of man.

(For the sparrow flies unthinking
And quarrels in his flight;
The heron trails his legs behind,
The lark goes out of sight;
But the great and flashing magpie
He flies as poets might.)

T. P. CAMERON WILSON
killed in action, 1918

Soliloquy

When I was young I had a care
Lest I should cheat me of my share
Of that which makes it sweet to strive
For life, and dying still survive,
A name in sunshine written higher
Than lark or poet dare aspire.

But I grew weary doing well,
Besides, 'twas sweeter in that hell,
Down with the loud banditti people
Who robbed the orchards, climbed the steeple
For jackdaws' eggs and made the cock
Crow ere 'twas daylight on the clock.
I was so very bad the neighbours
Spoke of me at their daily labours.

And now I'm drinking wine in France,
The helpless child of circumstance.
Tomorrow will be loud with war,
How will I be accounted for?

It is too late now to retrieve
A fallen dream, too late to grieve
A name unmade, but not too late
To thank the gods for what is great;
A keen-edged sword, a soldier's heart,
Is greater than a poet's art.
And greater than a poet's fame
A little grave that has no name.

FRANCIS LEDWIDGE
killed in action, 1917

Before Action

By all the glories of the day
  And the cool evening's benison,
By that last sunset touch that lay
  Upon the hills when day was done,
By beauty lavishly outpoured
  And blessings carelessly received,
By all the days that I have lived
  Make me a soldier, Lord.

By all of man's hopes and fears,
  And all the wonders poets sing,
The laughter of unclouded years,
  And every sad and lovely thing;
By the romantic ages stored
  With high endeavour that was his,
By all his mad catastrophes
  Make me a man, O Lord.

I, that on my familiar hill
  Saw with uncomprehending eyes
A hundred of Thy sunsets spill
  Their fresh and sanguine sacrifice,

Ere the sun swings his noonday sword
   Must say goodbye to all of this; –
By all delights that I shall miss,
   Help me to die, O Lord.

                W. N. HODGSON
             written two days before his
             death on July 1st, 1916

The Aisne

We saw fire on the tragic slopes
Where the flood-tide of France's early gain,
Big with wrecked promise and abandoned hopes,
Broke in a surf of blood along the Aisne.

The charge her heroes left us, we assumed,
What, dying, they reconquered, we preserved,
In the chill trenches, harried, shelled, entombed,
Winter came down on us, but no man swerved.

Winter came down on us. The low clouds, torn
In the stark branches of the riven pines,
Blurred the white rockets that from dusk till morn
Traced the wide curve of the close-grappling lines.

In rain, and fog that on the withered hill
Froze before dawn, the lurking foe drew down;
Or light snows fell that made forlorner still
The ravaged country and the ruined town;

Or the long clouds would end. Intensely fair,
The winter constellations blazing forth –
Pursues, the Twins, Orion, the Great Bear –
Gleamed on our bayonets pointing to the north.

And the lone sentinel would start and soar
On wings of strong emotion as he knew
That kinship with the stars that only War
Is great enough to lift man's spirit to.

And ever down the curving front, aglow
With the pale rockets' intermittent light,
He heard, like distant thunder, growl and grow
The rumble of far battles in the night, –

Rumours, reverberant, indistinct, remote,
Borne from red fields whose martial names have won
The power to thrill like a far trumpet-note, –
Vic, Vailly, Soupir, Hurtelise, Craonne . . .

Craonne, before thy cannon-swept plateau,
Where like sere leaves lay strewn September's dead,
I found for all things I forfeited
A recompense I would not forgo.

For that high fellowship was ours then
With those who, championing another's good,
More than dull Peace or its poor votaries could,
Taught us the dignity of being men.

There we drained deeper the deep cup of life,
And on sublimer summits came to learn,
After soft things, the terrible and stern,
After sweet Love, the majesty of Strife;

There where we faced under those frowning heights
The blast that maims, the hurricane that kills;
There where the watch-lights on the winter hills
Flickered like balefire through inclement nights;

There where, firm links in the unyielding chain,
Where fell the long-planned blow and fell in vain –
Hearts worthy of the honour and the trial,
We helped to hold the lines along the Aisne.

ALAN SEEGER

Rendezvous

I have a rendezvous with Death
At some disputed barricade,
When Spring comes back with rustling shade
And apple-blossoms fill the air –
I have a rendezvous with Death
When Spring brings back blue days and fair.

It may be he shall take my hand
And lead me into his dark land
And close my eyes and quench my breath –
It may be I shall pass him still.
I have a rendezvous with Death
On some scarred slope of battered hill,
When Spring comes round again this year
And the first meadow-flowers appear.

God knows 'twere better to be deep
Pillowed in silk and scented down,
Where love throbs out in blissful sleep,
Pulse nigh to pulse, and breath to breath,
Where hushed awakenings are dear . . .
But I've a rendezvous with Death
At midnight in some flaming town,
When Spring trips north again this year,
And I to my pledged word am true,
I shall not fail that rendezvous.

ALAN SEEGER
killed in action, 1916

A Listening Post

The sun's a red ball in the oak
   And all the grass is grey with dew,
Awhile ago a blackbird spoke –
   He didn't know the world's askew.

And yonder rifleman and I
   Wait here behind the misty trees
To shoot the first man that goes by,
   Our rifles ready on our knees.

How could he know that if we fail
   The world may lie in chains for years
And England be a bygone tale
   And right be wrong, and laughter tears?

Strange that this bird sits there and sings
   While we must only sit and plan –
Who are so much the higher things –
   The murder of our fellow man . . .

But maybe God will cause to be –
   Who brought forth sweetness from the strong –
Out of our discords harmony
   Sweeter than that bird's song.

                R. E. VERNÈDE
             killed in action, 1917

Before the Summer

When our men are marching lightly up and down,
When the pipes are playing through the little town,
I see a thin line swaying through wind and mud and rain
And the broken regiments come back to rest again.

Now the pipes are playing, now the drums are beat,
Now the strong battalions are marching up the street,
But the pipes will not be playing and the bayonets will not shine,
When the regiments I dream of come stumbling down the line.

Between the battered trenches their silent dead will lie
Quiet with grave eyes staring at the summer sky.
There is a mist upon them so that I cannot see
The faces of my friends that walk the little town with me.

Lest we see a worse thing than it is to die,
Live ourselves and see our friends cold beneath the sky,
God grant we too be lying there in wind and mud and rain
Before the broken regiments come stumbling back again.

> E. A. MACKINTOSH
> *1916, before the Somme battle*

Into Battle

The naked earth is warm with spring,
   And with green grass and bursting trees
Leans to the sun's gaze glorying,
   And quivers in the sunny breeze;
And life is colour and warmth and light,
   And a striving evermore for these;
And he is dead who will not fight;
   And who dies fighting has increase.

The fighting man shall from the sun
   Take warmth, and life from the glowing earth;
Speed with the light-foot winds to run,
   And with the trees to newer birth;
And find, when fighting shall be done,
   Great rest, and fullness after dearth.

All the bright company of Heaven
   Hold him in their high comradeship,
The Dog-Star, and the Sisters Seven,
   Orion's Belt and sworded hip.

The woodland trees that stand together,
   They stand to him each one a friend;
They gently speak in the windy weather;
   They guide to valley and ridge's end.

The kestrel hovering by day,
   And the little owls that call by night,
Bid him be swift and keen as they,
   As keen of ear, as swift of sight.

The blackbird sings to him, 'Brother, brother,
   If this be the last song you shall sing,
Sing well, for you may not sing another;
   Brother, sing.'

In dreary, doubtful, waiting hours,
   Before the brazen frenzy starts,
The horses show him nobler powers;
   O patient eyes, courageous hearts!

And when the burning moment breaks,
   And all things else are out of mind,
And only joy of battle takes
   Him by the throat, and makes him blind,

Through joy and blindness he shall know,
   Not caring much to know, that still
Nor lead nor steel shall reach him, so
   That it be not the Destined Will.

The thundering line of battle stands,
  And in the air death moans and sings;
But Day shall clasp him with strong hands,
  And Night shall fold him in soft wings.

JULIAN GRENFELL
died of wounds, 1915

In the Grass: Halt by Roadside

In my tired, helpless body
I feel my sunk heart ache;
But suddenly, loudly
The far, great guns shake.

Is it sudden terror
Burdens my heart? My hand
Flies to my head. I listen . . .
And do not understand.

Is death so near, then?
From this blaze of light
Do I plunge suddenly
Into Vortex? Night?

Guns again! the quiet
Shakes at the vengeful voice . . .
It is terrible pleasure.
I do not fear: I rejoice.

ROBERT NICHOLS

Noon

It is midday: the deep trench glares . . .
A buzz and blaze of flies . . .
The hot wind puffs the giddy airs . . .
The great sun rakes the skies.

No sound in all the stagnant trench
Where forty standing men
Endure the sweat and grit and stench,
Like cattle in a pen.

Sometimes a sniper's bullet whirs
Or twangs the whining wire;
Sometimes a soldier sighs and stirs
As in hell's frying fire.

From out a high cool cloud descends
An aeroplane's far moan . . .
The sun strikes down, the thin cloud rends . . .
The black spot travels on.

And sweating, dizzied, isolate
In the hot trench beneath,
We bide the next shrewd move of fate
Be it of life or death.

ROBERT NICHOLS

Eve of Assault: Infantry Going Down to Trenches

Downward slopes the wild red sun.
We lie around a waiting gun;
Soon we shall load and fire and load.
But, hark! a sound beats down the road.

"Ello! wot's up?' 'Let's 'ave a look!'
'Come on, Ginger, drop that book!'
'Wot an 'ell of bloody noise!'
'It's the Yorks and Lancs, meboys!'

So we crowd: hear, watch them come –
One man drubbing on a drum,
A crazy, high mouth-organ blowing,
Tin cans rattling, cat-calls, crowing . . .

And above their rhythmic feet
A whirl of shrilling loud and sweet,
Round mouths whistling in unison;
Shouts: "O's goin' to out the 'Un?'

'Back us up, mates!' 'Gawd, we will!'
"Eave them shells at Kaiser Bill!'
'Art from Lancashire, melad?'
'Gi' 'en a cheer, boys; make 'en glad.'

"Ip 'urrah!' 'Give Fritz the chuck.'
'Good ol' bloody Yorks!' 'Good-luck!'
'Cheer!'

I cannot cheer or speak
Lest my voice, my heart must break.
ROBERT NICHOLS

Comrades: an Episode

Before, before he was aware
The 'Verey' light had risen . . . on the air
It hung glistering . . .
                    And he could not stay his hand
From moving to the barbed wire's broken strand.
A rifle cracked.
                    He fell.
Night waned. He was alone. A heavy shell
Whispered itself passing high, high overhead.

His wound was wet to his hand: for still it bled
On to the glimmering ground.
Then with a slow, vain smile his wound he bound,
Knowing, of course, he'd not see home again –
Home whose thought he put away.
                                        His men
Whispered: 'Where's Mister Gates?' 'Out on the wire.'
'I'll get him,' said one . . .
                                Dawn blinked, and the fire
Of the Germans heaved up and down the line.
'Stand to!'
                    Too late! 'I'll get him.' 'O the swine!
When we might get him in yet safe and whole!'
'Corporal didn't see 'un fall out on patrol,
Or he'd 'a got 'un.' 'Sssh!'
                                'No talking there.'
A whisper: ''A went down at the last flare.'
Meanwhile the Maxims toc-toc-tocked; their swish
Of bullets told death lurked against the wish.
No hope for him!
                        His corporal, as one shamed,
Vainly and helplessly his ill-luck blamed.

Then Gates slowly saw the morn
Break in a rosy peace through the lone thorn
By which he lay, and felt the dawn-wind pass
Whispering through the pallid, stalky grass
Of No-Man's Land . . .
                        And the tears came
Scaldingly sweet, more lovely than a flame.
He closed his eyes: he thought of home
And grit his teeth. He knew no help could come . . .

The silent sun over the earth held sway,
Occasional rifles cracked and far away

A heedless speck, a 'plane, slid on alone,
Like a fly traversing a cliff of stone.
'I must get back,' said Gates aloud, and heaved
At his body. But it lay bereaved
Of any power. He could not wait till night . . .
And he lay still. Blood swam across his sight.
Then with a groan:
'No luck ever! Well, I must die alone.'

Occasional rifles cracked. A cloud that shone,
Gold-rimmed, blackened the sun and then was gone . . .
The sun still smiled. The grass sang in its play.
Someone whistled: 'Over the hills and far away.'
Gates watched silently the swift, swift sun
Burning his life before it was begun . . .

Suddenly he heard Corporal Timmins' voice: 'Now then,
'Urry up with that tea.'
                        'Hi Ginger!' 'Bill!' His men!
Timmins and Jones and Wilkinson (the 'bard'),
And Hughes and Simpson. It was hard
Not to see them: Wilkinson, stubby, grim,
With his 'No, sir,' 'Yes, sir,' and the slim
Simpson: 'Indeed, sir?' (while it seemed he winked
Because his smiling left eye always blinked)
And Corporal Timmins, straight and blond and wise,
With his quiet-scanning, level, hazel eyes;
And all the others . . . tunics that didn't fit . . .
A dozen different sorts of eyes. O it
Was hard to lie there! Yet he must. But no:
'I've got to die. I'll get to them. I'll go.'

Inch by inch he fought, breathless and mute,
Dragging his carcase like a famished brute . . .

His head was hammering, and his eyes were dim;
A bloody sweat seemed to ooze out of him
And freeze along his spine . . . Then he'd lie still
Before another effort of his will
Took him one nearer yard.
                              The parapet was reached.
He could not rise to it. A lookout screeched:
'Mr Gates!'
                Three figures in one breath
Leaped up. Two figures fell in toppling death;
And Gates was lifted in. 'Who's hit?' said he.
'Timmins and Jones.' 'Why did they that for me? –
I'm gone already!' Gently they laid him prone
And silently watched.
                        He twitched. They heard him moan

'Why for me?' His eyes roamed round, and none replied.
'I see it was alone I should have died.'
They shook their heads. Then, 'Is the doctor here?'
'He's coming, sir; he's hurryin', no fear.'
'No good . . .
                Lift me.' They lifted him.
He smiled and held his arms out to the dim,
And in a moment passed beyond their ken,
Hearing him whisper, 'O my men, my men!'

                                ROBERT NICHOLS

Youth at Arms

XVII

Now in the darkness Rum, the hearty priest,
Has laid his unction to my troops; they wet
Their lips and crouch against the parapet,
Where each fixed sword impales the greying east.

Excited laughs and bragging threats to drive
Old Jerry's end in tell me that their heart
For this hour seizes with true poet's art
The challenge and adventure of man's life,
Bitter and lovely, fugitive and strange.
At last the barrage roars its opening range.
The air's a cloud of shell-fumes and the stench
Of new-churned graves. We surge up from the trench.
My runner's breath smokes white in the dawn-mist yellow,
And a flare lights up on his eyebrow some beads of dew.
I grin to my heart and whisper, All's well, old fellow,
Today you are good for whatever is up to you.

LEONARD BARNES

Come on, My Lucky Lads

O rosy red, O torrent splendour
    Staining all the Orient gloom,
O celestial work of wonder –
    A million mornings in one bloom!

What, does the artist of creation
    Try some new plethora of flame,
For his eye's fresh fascination?
    Has the old cosmic fire grown tame?

In what subnatural strange awaking
    Is this body, which seems mine?
These feet towards that blood-burst making,
    These ears which thunder, these hands which twine

On grotesque iron? Icy-clear
    The air of a mortal day shocks sense,
My shaking men pant after me here.
    The acid vapours hovering dense,

The fury whizzing in dozens down,
   The clattering rafters, clods calcined,
The blood in the flints and the trackway brown –
   I see I am clothed and in my right mind;

The dawn but hangs behind the goal,
   What is that artist's joy to me?
Here limps poor Jock with a gash in the poll,
   His red blood now is the red I see,

The swooning white of him, and that red!
   These bombs in boxes, the craunch of shells,
The second-hand flitting round; ahead!
   It's plain we were born for this, naught else.

EDMUND BLUNDEN

Chemin des Dames

In silks and satins the ladies went
Where the breezes sighed and the poplars bent,
Taking the air of a Sunday morn
Midst the red of poppies and gold of corn –
Flowery ladies in stiff brocades,
With negro pages and serving-maids,
In scarlet coach or in gilt sedan,
With brooch and buckle and flounce and fan,
Patch and powder and trailing scent,
Under the trees the ladies went –
Lovely ladies that gleamed and glowed,
As they took the air on the Ladies' Road.

Boom of thunder and lightning flash –
The torn earth rocks to the barrage crash;
The bullets whine and the bullets sing
From the mad machine-guns chattering;

Black smoke rolling across the mud,
Trenches plastered with flesh and blood –
The blue ranks lock with the ranks of grey,
Stab and stagger and sob and sway;
The living cringe from the shrapnel bursts,
The dying moan of their burning thirsts,
Moan and die in the gulping slough –
Where are the butterfly ladies now?

CROSBIE GARSTIN
written during the action of Chemin des Dames

This is no Case of Petty Right or Wrong

This is no case of petty right or wrong
That politicians or philosophers
Can judge. I hate not Germans, nor grow hot
With love of Englishmen, to please newspapers.
Beside my hate for one fat patriot
My hatred of the Kaiser is love true: –
A kind of god he is, banging a gong.
But I have not to choose between the two,
Or between justice and injustice. Dinned
With war and argument I read no more
Than in the storm smoking along the wind
Athwart the wood. Two witches' cauldrons roar.
From one the weather shall rise clear and gay;
Out of the other an England beautiful
And like her mother that died yesterday.
Little I know or care if, being dull,
I shall miss something that historians
Can rake out of the ashes when perchance
The phoenix broods serene above their ken.
But with the best and meanest Englishmen
I am one in crying, God save England, lest

We lose what never slaves and cattle blessed.
The ages made her that made us from dust:
She is all we know and live by, and we trust
She is good and must endure, loving her so:
And as we love ourselves we hate our foe.

EDWARD THOMAS

Before the Charge

The night is still and the air is keen,
    Tense with menace the time crawls by,
In front is the town and its homes are seen,
    Blurred in outline against the sky.
The dead leaves float in the sighing air,
    The darkness moves like a curtain drawn,
A veil which the morning sun will tear
    From the face of death. – We charge at dawn.

PATRICK MACGILL

Untitled

When you see millions of the mouthless dead
Across your dreams in pale battalions go,
Say not soft things as other men have said,
That you'll remember. For you need not so.
Give them not praise. For, deaf, how should they know
It is not curses heaped on each gashed head?
Nor tears. The blind eyes see not your tears flow.
Nor honour. It is easy to be dead.
Say only this, 'They are dead.' Then add thereto,
'Yet many a better one has died before.'
Then, scanning all the o'ercrowded mass, should you

Perceive one face that you loved heretofore,
It is a spook. None wears the face you knew.
Great death has made all his for evermore.

                                    C. H. SORLEY

To Germany

You are blind like us. Your hurt no man designed,
And no man claimed the conquest of your land.
But gropers both through fields of thought confined
We stumble and we do not understand.
You only saw your future bigly planned,
And we, the tapering paths of our own mind,
And in each other's dearest ways we stand,
And hiss and hate. And the blind fight the blind.

When it is peace, then we may view again
With new-won eyes each other's truer form
And wonder. Grown more loving-kind and warm
We'll grasp firm hands and laugh at the old pain,
When it is peace. But until peace, the storm
The darkness and the thunder and the rain.

                                    C. H. SORLEY

Flanders

Man has the life of butterflies
In the sunshine of sacrifice;
Brief and brilliant, but more
Guerdon than the honeyed flower,
And more glory than the grace
Of their gentle floating pace.

                        WILLOUGHBY WEAVING

From a Flemish Graveyard

A year hence may the grass that waves
O'er English men in Flemish graves,
Coating this clay with green of peace
And softness of a year's increase,
Be kind and lithe as English grass
To bend and nod as the winds pass;
It was for grass on English hills
These bore too soon the last of ills.

And may the wind be brisk and clean,
And singing cheerfully between
The bents a pleasant-burdened song
To cheer these English dead along;
For English songs and English winds
Are they that bred these English minds.

And may the circumstantial trees
Dip, for these dead ones, in the breeze,
And make for them their silver play
Of spangled boughs each shiny day.
Thus may these look above, and see
And hear the wind in grass and tree,
And watch a lark in heaven stand,
And think themselves in their own land.

                              I. A. WILLIAMS

The Dead

Blow out, you bugles, over the rich Dead!
    There's none of these so lonely and poor of old,
But, dying, has made us rarer gifts than gold.

These laid the world away; poured out the red
Sweet wine of youth; gave up the years to be
　　Of work and joy, and that unhoped serene,
　　That men call age; and those who would have been,
Their sons, they gave, their immortality.

Blow, bugles, blow! They brought us, for our dearth,
　　Holiness, lacked so long, and Love, and Pain,
Honour has come back, as a king, to earth,
　　And paid his subjects with a royal wage;
And nobleness walks in our ways again;
　　And we have come into our heritage.

RUPERT BROOKE

The Anxious Dead

O Guns, fall silent till the dead men hear
　　Above their heads the legions pressing on:
(These fought their fight in time of bitter fear,
　　And died not knowing how the day had gone.)

O flashing muzzles, pause, and let them see
　　The coming dawn that streaks the sky afar;
Then let your mighty chorus witness be
　　To them, and Ceasar, that we still make war.

Tell them, O guns, that we have heard their call,
　　That we have sworn and will not turn aside,
That we will onward till we win or fall,
　　That we will keep the faith for which they died.

Bid them be patient, and some day, anon,
　　They shall feel earth enwrapt in silence deep;
Shall greet, in wonderment, the quiet dawn,
　　And in content may turn them to their sleep.

JOHN MCCRAE

In Flanders Fields

In Flanders fields the poppies blow
Between the crosses, row on row
    That mark our place; and in the sky
    The larks, still bravely singing, fly
Scarce heard amid the guns below.

We are the Dead. Short days ago
We lived, felt dawn, saw sunset glow,
    Loved and were loved, and now we lie
    In Flanders fields.

Take up our quarrel with the foe:
To you from failing hands we throw
    The torch; be yours to hold it high.
    If ye break faith with us who die
We shall not sleep, though poppies grow
    In Flanders fields.

JOHN MCRAE
died in Base Hospital, 1918

To Unknown Lands

We are the R.F.C.
We cannot fight
We cannot shoot
What blinking use are we?
But when we reach Berlin
The Kaiser he will say
Mein Gott! Mein Gott!
What a jolly fine lot
Are the boys of the R.F.C.

SONG

An Irish Airman foresees his Death

I know that I shall meet my fate
Somewhere among the clouds above;
Those that I fight I do not hate,
Those that I guard I do not love;
My country is Kiltartan Cross,
My countrymen Kiltartan's poor,
No likely end could bring them loss
Or leave them happier than before.
Nor law, nor duty bade me fight,
Nor public men, nor cheering crowds,
A lonely impulse of delight
Drove to this tumult in the clouds;
I balanced all, brought all to mind,
The years to come seemed waste of breath,
A waste of breath the years behind
In balance with this life, this death.

W. B. YEATS

On the Wings of the Morning

A sudden roar, a mighty rushing sound,
    a jolt or two, a smoothly sliding rise,
a tumbled blur of disappearing ground,
    and then all sense of motion slowly dies.
        Quiet and calm, the earth slips past below,
        as underneath a bridge still waters flow.

My turning wing inclines towards the ground;
    The ground itself glides up with graceful swing
and at the plane's far tip twirls slowly round,
    then drops from sight again beneath the wing
        to slip away serenely as before,
        a cubist-patterned carpet on the floor

Hills gently sink and valleys gently fill.
　　The flattened fields grow ludicrously small;
slowly they pass beneath and slower still
　　until they hardly seem to move at all.
　　　　Then suddenly they disappear from sight,
　　　　hidden by fleeting wisps of faded white.

The wing-tips, faint and dripping, dimly show,
　　blurred by the wreaths of mist that intervene.
Weird, half-seen shadows flicker to and fro
　　across the pallid fog-bank's blinding screen.
　　　　At last the choking mists release their hold,
　　　　and all the world is silver, blue, and gold.

The air is clear, more clear than sparkling wine;
　　compared with this, wine is a turgid brew.
The far horizon makes a clean-cut line
　　between the silver and the depthless blue.
　　　　Out of the snow-white level reared on high
　　　　glittering hills surge up to meet the sky.

Outside the wind screen's shelter gales may race:
　　but in the seat a cool and gentle breeze
blows steadily upon my grateful face.
　　As I sit motionless and at my ease,
　　　　contented just to loiter in the sun
　　　　and gaze around me till the day is done.

And so I sit, half sleeping, half awake,
　　dreaming a happy dream of golden days,
until at last, with a reluctant shake
　　I rouse myself, and with a lingering gaze
　　　　at all the splendour of the shining plain
　　　　make ready to come down to earth again.

The engine stops: a pleasant silence reigns –
   silence, not broken, but intensified
by the soft, sleepy wires' insistent strains,
      that rise and fall, as with a sweeping glide
         I slither down the well-oiled sides of space,
         towards a lower, less enchanted place.

The clouds draw nearer, changing as they come.
   Now, like a flash, fog grips me by the throat.
Down goes the nose: at once the wires' low hum
      begins to rise in volume and in note,
         till, as I hurtle from the choking cloud
         it swells into a scream, high-pitched, and loud.

The scattered hues and shades of green and brown
   fashion themselves into the land I know,
turning and twisting, as I spiral down
      towards the landing-ground; till, skimming low,
         I glide with slackening speed across the ground,
         and come to rest with lightly grating sound.

JEFFERY DAY
killed in action, 1918

Nox Mortis

The afternoon
   Flutters and dies:
The fairy moon
   Burns in the skies
As they grow darker, and the first stars shine
On Night's rich mantle – purple like warm wine.

On each white road
Begins to crawl
The heavy toad:
The night-birds call,
And round the trees the swift bats flit and wheel,
While from the barns the rats begin to steal.

So now must I,
Bird of the night,
Towards the sky
Make wheeling flight,
And bear my poison o'er the gloomy land,
And let it loose with hard unsparing hand.

The chafers boom
With whirring wings,
And haunt the gloom
Which twilight brings –
So in nocturnal travel do I wail
As through the night the wingèd engines sail.

Death, Grief, and Pain
Are what I give.
O that the slain
Might live – might live!
I know them not, for I have blindly killed,
And nameless hearts with nameless sorrow filled.

Thrice cursèd War
Which bids that I
Such death should pour
Down from the sky.
O, Star of Peace, rise swiftly in the East
That from such slaying men may be released.

PAUL BEWSHER

Outward Bound

There's a waterfall I'm leaving
Running down the rocks in foam,
There's a pool for which I'm grieving
Near the water-ouzel's home,
And it's there that I'd be lying
With the heather close at hand,
And the curlews faintly crying
Mid the wastes of Cumberland.

While the midnight watch is winging
Thoughts of other days arise,
I can hear the river singing
Like the Saints in Paradise;
I can see the water winking
Like the merry eyes of Pan,
And the slow half-pounder sinking
By the bridge's granite span.

Ah! to win them back and clamber
Braced anew with winds I love,
From the river's stainless amber
To the morning mist above,
See through cloud-rifts rent asunder
Like a painted scroll unfurled,
Ridge and hollow rolling under
To the fringes of the world.

Now the weary guard are sleeping,
Now the great propellers churn,
Now the harbour lights are creeping
Into emptiness astern,

While the sentry wakes and watches
Plunging triangles of light
Where the water leaps and catches
At our escort in the night.

Great their happiness who seeing
Still with unbenighted eyes
Kin of theirs who gave them being,
Sun and earth that made them wise,
Die and feel their embers quicken
Year by year in summer time,
When the cotton grasses thicken
On the hills they used to climb.

Shall we also be as they be,
Mingled with our mother clay,
Or return no more it may be?
Who has knowledge, who shall say?
Yet we hope that from the bosom
Of our shaggy father Pan,
When the earth breaks into blossom
Richer from the dust of man,

Though the high Gods smite and slay us,
Though we come not whence we go,
As the host of Menelaus
Came there many years ago;
Yet the self-same wind shall bear us
From the same departing place
Out across the Gulf of Saros
And the peaks of Samothrace;

We shall pass in summer weather,
We shall come at eventide,
When the fells stand up together
And all quiet things abide;

Mixed with cloud and wind and river,
Sun-distilled in dew and rain,
One with Cumberland for ever
We shall go not forth again.

NOWELL OXLAND
killed in action, Gallipoli, 1915

Untitled

I saw a man this morning
    Who did not wish to die:
I ask, and cannot answer,
    If otherwise wish I.

Fair broke the day this morning
    Against the Dardanelles;
The breeze blew soft, the morn's cheeks
    Were cold as cold sea-shells.

But other shells are waiting
    Across the Aegean Sea,
Shrapnel and high explosive,
    Shells and hells for me.

O hell of ships and cities,
    Hell of men like me,
Fatal second Helen,
    Why must I follow thee?

Achilles came to Troyland
    And I to Chersonese:
He turned from wrath to battle,
    And I from three days' peace.

Was it so hard, Achilles,
   So very hard to die?
Thou knowest and I know not –
   So much the happier am I.

I will go back this morning
   From Imbros over the sea;
Stand in the trench, Achilles,
   Flame-capped, and shout for me.

PATRICK SHAW-STEWART
Gallipoli; killed in action, 1917

From 'W' Beach

The Isle of Imbros, set in turquoise blue,
   Lies to the westward; on the eastern side
The purple hills of Asia fade from view,
   And rolling battleships at anchor ride.

White flocks of cloud float by, the sunset glows,
   And dipping gulls fleck a slow-waking sea,
Where dim steel-shadowed forms with foaming bows
   Wind up in the Narrows towards Gallipoli.

No colour breaks this tongue of barren land
   Save where a group of huddled tents gleams white;
Before me ugly shapes like spectres stand,
   And wooden crosses cleave the waning light.

Now the sky gardeners speed the hurrying day
   And sow the plains of night with silver grain;
So shall this transient havoc fade away
   And the proud cape be beautiful again.

Laden with figs and olives, or a freight
   Of purple grapes, tanned singing men shall row,
Chanting wild songs of how Eternal Fate
   Withstood that fierce invasion long ago.

GEOFFREY DEARMER
Gallipoli

From *The Dug-out; A Memory of Gallipoli*

There, where the sun, the senseless sun
         kept pouring,
  And dust-clouds smothered one
          about the chest,
While secret waters filtered through the flooring
  (In case the heat should leave one *too* oppressed),
Always I lay in those sad fevered seasons
Which Red-hot humorists, for mystic reasons,
  Regarded as our 'rest'.

A. P. HERBERT

The Gift

Marching on Tanga, marching the parch'd plain
Of wavering spear-grass past the Pangani River,
England came to me – me who had always ta'en
But never given before – England, the giver,
In a vision of three poplar-trees that shiver
On still evenings of summer, after rain,
By Slapton Ley, where reed-beds start and quiver
Where scarce a ripple moves the upland grain.
Then I thanked God that now I had suffered pain
And, as the parch'd plain, thirst, and lain awake

Shivering all night through till cold daybreak:
In that I count these sufferings my gain
And her acknowledgment. Nay, more, would fain
Suffer as many more for her sweet sake.

FRANCIS BRETT YOUNG
in German East Africa

After Action

All through that day of battle the broken sound
Of shattering Maxim fire made mad the wood;
So that the low trees shuddered where they stood,
And echoes bellowed in the bush around:
But when, at last, the light of day was drowned,
That madness ceased . . . Ah, God, but it was good!
There in the reek of iodine and blood,
I flung me down upon the thorny ground.
So quiet was it, I might well have been lying
In a room I love, where the ivy cluster shakes
Its dew upon the lattice panes at even:
Where rusty ivory scatters from the dying
Jessamine blossom, and the musk-rose breaks
Her dusky bloom beneath a summer heaven.

FRANCIS BRETT YOUNG

Prisoners

Prisoners of risk and rigour long ago
Who have done battle under honour's name,
Hoped (living or shot down) some meed of fame,
And wooed bright Danger for a thrilling kiss, –
Laugh, oh laugh well, that we have come to this!

Laugh, oh laugh loud, all ye who long ago
Adventure found in gallant company!
Safe in Stagnation, laugh, laugh bitterly,
While on this filthiest backwater of Time's flow
Drift we and rot, till something set us free!

Laugh like old men with senses atrophied,
Heeding no Present, to the Future dead,
Nodding quite foolish by the warm fireside
And seeing no flame, but only in the red
And flickering embers, pictures of the past: —
Life like a cinder fading black at last.

F. W. HARVEY
in a Prisoner-of-War camp

Barbed Wire

What bramble thicket this – grown overnight
on the clean earth – unflowering? In the dusk,
some mad end, loosened, taps upon its pole:
thorns tapping like the ghosts of dead delight.

Wire, barbed wire! – A dour
and monstrous serpent round our lives,
and we're like creatures mesmerized;
it glares at us, all day, malignant, sour.

Wire – fifteen feet of crouching coils to lock
man out from Heaven's wonder!
And yet, each evening, grey moths come to mock
and conjure it asunder.

A No Man's Land, where little things can creep
and love and dance together;
flowers live ensanctuaried and crickets 'cheep';
birds sing in silent weather.

Wire – in Winter-time the snow
comes writhing down to perch on it
in great festoons. White-tented, now,
the distance marches in a bit.

R. H. SAUTER
in a Prisoner-of-War camp

The Wadi

Wind that in the Wadi
Sett'st the scrub asighing,
In the Wadi, where the grouse are crying!
Like the souls of men
Homeward fleeting,
Through the wintry heavens the fowl their way are beating.

Stream that in the Wadi
Sett'st the grass aswaying,
In the Wadi, where the waves are playing!
Like the souls of men
Homeward going,
Down the racing stream the silvered waves are flowing.

You that saw men die,
Wind and Stream! Reply!
After all our pain
Does no trace remain, –
None; but flying
Wings, and crying
Fowl, and weeds and water sighing?

EDWARD THOMPSON
after the action of
January 13th, 1916, Mesopotamia

The Forest of the Dead

There are strange trees in that pale field
Of barren soil and bitter yield:
They stand without the city walls;
Their nakedness is unconcealed.

Cross after cross, mound after mound,
And no flowers blossom but are bound,
The dying and the dead, in the wreaths
Sad crowns for kings of Underground.

The forest of the dead is still,
No song of birds can ever thrill
Among the sapless boughs that bear
No fruit, no flower, for good or ill.

The sun by day, the moon by night
Give terrible or tender light,
But night or day the forest stands
Unchanging, desolately bright.

With loving or unloving eye
Kinsman and alien pass them by:
Do the dead know, do the dead care,
Under the forest as they lie?

To each the tree above his head,
To each the sign in which is said . . .
'By this thou art to overcome':
Under this forest sleep no dead.

These, having life, gave life away:
Is God less generous than they?
The spirit passes and is free:
Dust to the dust; Death takes the clay.

J. GRIFFYTH FAIRFAX
Mesopotamia

Mesopotamia

They shall not return to us, the resolute, the young,
    The eager and whole-hearted whom we gave:
But the men who left them thriftily to lie in their own dung,
    Shall they come with years and honour to the grave?

They shall not return to us, the strong men coldly slain
    In sight of help denied from day to day:
But the men who edged their agonies and chid them in their pain,
    Are they too strong and wise to put away?

Our dead shall not return to us while Day and Night divide –
    Never while the bars of sunset hold.
But the idle-minded overlings who quibbled while they died,
    Shall they thrust for high employments as of old?

Shall we only threaten and be angry for an hour?
    When the storm is ended shall we find
How softly but how swiftly they have sidled back to power
    By the favour and contrivance of their kind?

Even while they sooth us, while they promise large amends,
    Even while they make a show of fear,
Do they call upon their debtors, and take counsel with their friends,
    To confirm and re-establish each career?

Their lives cannot repay us – their death could not undo –
  The shame that they have laid upon our race.
But the slothfulness that wasted and the arrogance that slew,
  Shall we leave it unabated in its place?

RUDYARD KIPLING

1917

Troopship: mid-Atlantic

Dark waters into crystalline brilliance break
About the keel as, through the moonless night,
The dark ship moves in its own moving lake
Of phosphorescent cold moon-coloured light;
And to the clear horizon all around
Drift pools of fiery beryl flashing bright,
As though unquenchably burning cold and white
A million moons in the night of waters drowned.

And staring at the magic with eyes adream
That never till now have looked upon the sea,
Boys from the Middle West lounge listlessly
In the unlanthorned darkness, boys who go,
Beckoned by some unchallengeable dream,
To unknown lands to fight an unknown foe.

WILFRID GIBSON

on the S.S. Baltic, *July 1917*

From *Tulips and Chimneys*

the bigness of cannon
is skilful,

but i have seen
death's clever enormous voice
which hides in a fragility
of poppies . . .

i say that sometimes
on these long talkative animals
are laid fists of huger silence

I have seen all the silence
filled with vivid noiseless boys

at Roupy
i have seen
between barrages,

the night utter ripe unspeaking girls.

e. e. CUMMINGS

In the Dordogne

We stood up before day
and shaved by metal mirrors
in the faint flame of a faulty candle.

And we hurried down the wide stone stairs
with a clirr of spurr chains
on stone. And we thought
when the cocks crew
that the ghosts of a dead dawn
would rise and be off. But they stayed
under the window, crouched on the staircase,
the window now the colour of morning.

The colonel slept in the bed of Sully,
slept on: but we descended
and saw in a niche in the white wall
a Virgin and child, serene
who were stone: we saw sycamore:
three aged mages
scattering gifts of gold.

But when the wind blew, there were autumn odours
and the shadowed trees
had the dapplings of young fawns.

And each day one died or another
died: each week we sent out thousands
that returned by hundreds
wounded or gassed. And those that died
we buried close to the old wall
within a stone's throw of Perigord
under the tower of the troubadours.

And because we had courage;
because there was courage and youth
ready to be wasted; because we endured
and were prepared for all the endurance;
we thought something must come of it:
that the Virgin would raise her child and smile;
the trees gather up their gold and go;
that courage would avail something
and something we had never lost
be regained through wastage, by dying,
by burying the others under the English tower.

The colonel slept on in the bed of Sully
under the ravelling curtains: the leaves fell
and were blown away: the young men rotted
under the shadow of the tower
in a land of small clear silent streams
where the coming on of evening is
the letting down of blue and azure veils
over the clear and silent streams
delicately bordered by poplars.

                    JOHN PEALE BISHOP

Home Front

*

Take me back to dear old Blighty,
Put me on the train for London,
Take me over there . . .
Oh, tiddly-iddly-idee,
Hurry me home to Blighty,
Blighty is the place for me.

SONG

Bombed in London

On land and sea I strove with anxious care
To escape conscription. It was in the air!

RUDYARD KIPLING

Air-Raid

Night shatters in mid-heaven – the bark of guns,
The roar of planes, the crash of bombs, and all
The unshackled skyey pandemonium stuns
The senses to indifference, when a fall
Of masonry nearby startles awake,
Tingling, wide-eyed, prick-eared, with bristling hair,
Each sense within the body, crouched aware
Like some sore-hunted creature in the brake.

Yet side by side we lie in the little room,
Just touching hands, with eyes and ears that strain
Keenly, yet dream-bewildered, through tense gloom,
Listening, in helpless stupor of insane
Drugged nightmare panic fantastically wild,
To the quiet breathing of our little child.

WILFRID GIBSON

The Zeppelin

Guns! far and near,
Quick, sudden, angry,
They startle the still street.
Upturned faces appear,
Doors open on darkness,
There is a hurrying of feet,

And whirled athwart gloom
White fingers of alarm
Point at last there
Where illumined and dumb
A shape suspended
Hovers, a demon of the starry air!

Strange and cold as a dream
Of sinister fancy,
It charms like a snake,
Poised deadly in a gleam,
While bright explosions
Leap up to it and break.

Is it terror you seek
To exult in? Know then
Hearts are here
That the plunging beak
Of night-winged murder
Strikes not with fear

So much as it stings
To a deep elation
And a quivering pride
That at last the hour brings
For them too the danger
Of those who died,

Of those who yet fight,
Spending for each of us
Their glorious blood
In the foreign night, –
That now we are neared to them
Thank we God.

LAURENCE BINYON

The War Films

O living pictures of the dead,
  O songs without a sound,
O fellowship whose phantom tread
  Hallows a phantom ground –
How in a gleam have these revealed
  The faith we had not found.

We have sought God in a cloudy Heaven,
  We have passed by God on earth:
His seven sins and his sorrows seven,
  His wayworn mood and mirth,
Like a ragged cloak have hid from us
  The secret of his birth.

Brother of men, when now I see
  The lads go forth in line,
Thou knowest my heart is hungry in me
  As for thy bread and wine:
Thou knowest my heart is bowed in me
  To take their death for mine.

SIR HENRY NEWBOLT

The Miners' Response

*'We must keep on striking, striking, striking . . .' – from the
first speech by the Minister of Munitions.*

We do: the present desperate stage
Of fighting brings us luck;
And in the higher war we wage
(For higher wage) *We struck.*

D. S. MACCOLL

1915

The Verdicts

(Jutland)

Not in the thick of the fight,
  Not in the press of the odds,
Do the heroes come to their height,
  Or we know the demi-gods.

That stands over till peace.
  We can only perceive
Men returned from the seas,
  Very grateful for leave.

They grant us sudden days
  Snatched from their business of war;
But we are too close to appraise
  What manner of men they are.

And, whether their names go down
  With age-kept victories,
Or whether they battle and drown
  Unreckoned, is hid from our eyes.

They are too near to be great,
  But our children shall understand
When and how our fate
  Was changed, and by whose hand.

Our children shall measure their worth.
  We are content to be blind . . .
But we know that we walk on a new born earth
  With the saviours of mankind.

RUDYARD KIPLING

Mine-sweeping Trawlers

Not ours the fighter's glow,
   the glory, and the praise.
Unnoticed to and fro
   we pass our dangerous ways.

We sift the drifting sea,
   and blindly grope beneath;
obscure and toilsome we,
   the fishermen of death.

But when the great ships go
   to battle through the gloom,
our hearts beat high to know
   we cleared their path of doom.

E. HILTON YOUNG

Nineteen-fifteen

On a ploughland hill against the sky,
Over the barley, over the rye,
Time, which is now a black pine tree,
Holds out his arms and mocks at me –

'In the year of your Lord nineteen-fifteen
The acres are ploughed and the acres are green,
And the calves and the lambs and the foals are born,
But man the angel is all forlorn.

'The cropping cattle, the swallow's wing,
The wagon team and the pasture spring,
Move in their seasons and are most wise,
But man, whose image is in the skies,

'Who is master of all, whose hand achieves
The church and the barn and the homestead eaves –
How are the works of his wisdom seen
In the year of your Lord nineteen-fifteen?'

JOHN DRINKWATER

In Time of 'The Breaking of Nations'

Only a man harrowing clods
  In a slow silent walk
With an old horse that stumbles and nods
  Half asleep as they stalk.

Only thin smoke without flame
  From the heaps of couch-grass;
Yet this will go onward the same
  Though Dynasties pass.

Yonder a maid and her wight
  Come whispering by:
War's annals will cloud into night
  Ere their story die.

THOMAS HARDY

1915

Death's Kingdom

*

Send for the boys of the Old Brigade
To keep old England free!
Send for me father and me mother and me brother,
But for Gawd's sake don't send me.

*

If you want the old battalion,
We know where they are
– Hanging on the old barbed wire.

SONGS

Nightfall

Hooded in angry mist, the sun goes down:
Steel-gray the clouds roll out across the sea:
Is this a Kingdom? Then give Death the crown,
For here no emperor hath won, save He.

HERBERT ASQUITH
Sanctuary Wood, 1917

After the Salvo

Up and down, up and down,
They go, the gray rat, and the brown.
The telegraph lines are tangled hair,
Motionless on the sullen air;
An engine has fallen on its back,
With crazy wheels, on a twisted track;
All ground to dust is the little town;
Up and down, up and down
They go, the gray rat, and the brown.
A skull, torn out of the graves nearby,
Gapes in the grass. A butterfly,
In azure iridescence new,
Floats into the world, across the dew;
Between the flow'rs. Have we lost our way,
Or are we toys of a god at play,
Who do these things on a young Spring day?

Where the salvo fell, on a splintered ledge
Of ruin, at the crater's edge,
A poppy lives: and young, and fair,
The dewdrops hang on the spider's stair,
With every rainbow still unhurt
From leaflet unto leaflet girt.

Man's house is crushed; the spider's lives:
Inscrutably He takes, and gives,
Who guards not any temple here,
Save the temple of the gossamer.

Up and down, up and down
They go, the gray rat, and the brown:
A pistol cracks: they too are dead.

The nightwind rustles overhead.

HERBERT ASQUITH

From the Somme

In other days I sang of simple things,
  Of summer dawn, and summer noon and night,
The dewy grass, the dew-wet fairy rings,
  The larks long golden flight.

Deep in the forest I made melody
  While squirrels cracked their hazel nuts on high,
Or I would cross the wet sand to the sea
  And sing to sea and sky.

When came the silvered silence of the night
  I stole to casements over scented lawns,
And softly sang of love and love's delight
  To mute white marble fauns.

Oft in the tavern parlour I would sing
  Of morning sun upon the mountain vine,
And, calling for a chorus, sweep the string
  In praise of good red wine.

I played with all the toys the gods provide,
  I sang my songs and made glad holiday.
Now I have cast my broken toys aside
  And flung my lute away.

A singer once, I now am fain to weep.
  Within my soul I feel strange music swell,
Vast chants of tragedy too deep – too deep
  For my poor lips to tell.

LESLIE COULSON
killed in action, 1916

Bombardment

Four days the earth was rent and torn
By bursting steel,
The houses fell about us;
Three nights we dared not sleep,
Sweating, and listening for the imminent crash
Which meant our death.

The fourth night every man,
Nerve-tortured, racked to exhaustion,
Slept, muttering and twitching,
While the shells crashed overhead.

The fifth day there came a hush;
We left our holes
And looked above the wreckage of the earth
To where the white clouds moved in silent lines
Across the untroubled blue.

RICHARD ALDINGTON

Breakfast

We ate our breakfast lying on our backs
Because the shells were screeching overhead.
I bet a rasher to a loaf of bread
That Hull United would beat Halifax
When Jimmy Stainthorpe played full-back instead
Of Billy Bradford. Ginger raised his head
And cursed, and took the bet, and dropt back dead.
We ate our breakfast lying on our backs
Because the shells were screeching overhead.

WILFRID GIBSON

Mad

Neck-deep in mud,
He mowed and raved –
He who had braved
The field of blood –
And as a lad
Just out of school
Yelled – *April Fool!*
And laughed like mad.

WILFRID GIBSON

In the Ambulance

Two rows of cabbages,
Two of curly-greens,
Two rows of early peas,
Two of kidney-beans.

That's what he keeps muttering,
Making such a song,
Keeping other chaps awake
The whole night long.

Both his legs are shot away,
And his head is light,
So he keeps on muttering
All the blessed night:

Two rows of cabbages,
Two of curly-greens,
Two rows of early peas,
Two of kidney-beans.

WILFRID GIBSON

The Deserter

'I'm sorry I done it, Major.'
We bandaged the livid face;
And led him out, ere the wan sun rose,
To die his death of disgrace.

The bolt-heads locked to the cartridge;
The rifles steadied to rest,
As cold stock nestled at colder cheek
And foresight lined on the breast.

'*Fire!*' called the Sergeant-Major.
The muzzles flamed as he spoke:
And the shameless soul of a nameless man
Went up in the cordite-smoke.

GILBERT FRANKAU

From Albert to Bapaume

Lonely and bare and desolate,
Stretches of muddy filtered green,
A silence half articulate
Of all that those dumb eyes have seen.

A battered trench, a tree with boughs
Smutted and black with smoke and fire,
A solitary ruined house,
A crumpled mass of rusty wire.

And scarlet by each ragged fen
Long scattered ranks of poppies lay,
As though the blood of the dead men
Had not been wholly washed away.

ALEC WAUGH

Kismet

Opal fires in the Western sky
   (For that which is written must ever be),
And a bullet comes droning, whining by,
   To the heart of a sentry close to me.

For some go early, and some go late
   (A dying scream on the evening air)
And who is there that believes in Fate
   As a soul goes out in the sunset flare?

R. B. MARRIOTT-WATSON
killed in action, 1918

My Company

I

You became
In many acts and quiet observances
A body and a soul, entire.

I cannot tell
What time your life became mine:
Perhaps when one summer night
We halted on the roadside
In the starlight only,
And you sang your sad home-songs,
Dirges which I standing outside you
Coldly condemned.

Perhaps, one night, descending cold
When rum was mighty acceptable,
And my doling gave birth to sensual gratitude.

And then our fights: we've fought together
Compact, unanimous;
And I have felt the pride of leadership.

In many acts and quiet observances
You absorbed me:
Until one day I stood eminent
And I saw you gathered round me,
Uplooking,
And about you a radiance that seemed to beat
With variant glow and to give
Grace to our unity.

But, God! I know that I'll stand
Someday in the loneliest wilderness,
Someday my heart will cry
For the soul that has been, but that now
Is scatter'd with the winds,
Deceased and devoid.

I know that I'll wander with a cry:
'O beautiful men, O men I loved,
O whither are you gone, my company?'

2

My men go wearily
With their monstrous burdens.
They bear wooden planks
And iron sheeting
Through the area of death.

When a flare curves through the sky
They rest immobile.

Then on again,
Sweating and blaspheming –
'Oh, bloody Christ!'

My men, my modern Christs,
Your bloody agony confronts the world.

3

A man of mine
                lies on the wire.
It is death to fetch his soulless corpse.

A man of mine
                    lies on the wire;
And he will rot
And first his lips
The worms will eat.

It is not thus I would have him kiss'd,
But with the warm passionate lips
Of his comrade here.

4

I can assume
A giant attitude and godlike mood,
And then detachedly regard
All riots, conflicts and collisions.

The men I've lived with
Lurch suddenly into a far perspective;
They distantly gather like a dark cloud of birds
In the autumn sky.

Urged by some unanimous
Volition or fate,
Clouds clash in opposition;
The sky quivers, the dead descend;
Earth yawns.

They are all of one species.

From my giant attitude,
In godlike mood,
I laugh till space is filled
With hellish merriment.

Then again I resume
My human docility,
Bow my head
And share their doom.

HERBERT READ

'Trench Nomenclature'

Genius named them, as I live! What but genius could compress
In a title what man's humour said to man's supreme distress?
Jacob's Ladder ran reversed, from earth to a fiery pit extending
With not angels but poor Angles, those for the most part descending.
Thence *Brock's Benefit* commanded endless fireworks by two
    nations,
Yet some voices there were raised against the rival coruscations.
Picturedrome peeped out upon a dream, not Turner could surpass,
And presently the picture moved, and greyed with corpses and
    morass.
So down south; and if remembrance travel north, she marvels yet
At the sharp Shakespearian names, and with sad mirth her eyes are
    wet.
The Great Wall of China rose, a four-foot breast-work, fronting
    guns
That, when the word dropped, beat at once its silly ounces with
    brute tons;
Odd *Krab Krawl* on paper looks, and odd the foul-breathed alley
    twisted,
As one feared to twist there too, if *Minnie*, forward quean, insisted.
Where the Yser at *Dead End* floated on its bloody waters
Dead and rotten monstrous fish, note (east) *The Pike and Eel*
    headquarters.
Ah, such names and apparitions! name on name! what's in a name?
From the fabled vase the genie in his cloud of horror came.

EDMUND BLUNDEN

Premature Rejoicing

What's that over there?
                 Thiepval Wood.
Take a steady look at it; it'll do you good.
Here, these glasses will help you. See any flowers?
There sleeps Titania (correct – the Wood is ours);
There sleeps Titania in a deep dug-out,
Waking, she wonders what all the din's about,
And smiles through her tears, and looks ahead ten years
And sees her Wood again, and her usual Grenadiers,
      All in green,
      Music in the moon;
    The burnt rubbish you've just seen
    Won't beat the Fairy Queen;
      All the same, it's a shade too soon
      For you to scribble rhymes
      In your army book
      About those times;
      Take another look;
That's where the difficulty is, over there.

EDMUND BLUNDEN

Pill-box

Just see what's happening, Worley. – Worley rose
And round the angled doorway thrust his nose,
And Sergeant Hoad went too, to snuff the air.
Then war brought down his fist, and missed the pair!
Yet Hoad was scratched by a splinter, the blood came,
And out burst terrors that he'd striven to tame,
A good man, Hoad, for weeks. *I'm blown to bits.*

He groans, he screams. *Come, Bluffer, where's your wits?*
Says Worley. *Bluffer, you've a Blighty, man!*
All in the pill-box urged him, here began
His freedom: *Think of Eastbourne and your dad.*
The poor man lay at length and brief and mad
Flung out his cry of doom; soon ebbed and dumb
He yielded. Worley with a tot of rum
And shouting in his face could not restore him.
The ship of Charon over channel bore him.
All marvelled even on that most deathly day
To see this life so spirited away.

                                        EDMUND BLUNDEN

Winter Warfare

Colonel Cold strode up the Line
    (Tabs of rime and spurs of ice),
Stiffened all where he did glare,
    Horses, men, and lice.

Visited a forward post,
    Left them burning, ear to foot;
Fingers stuck to biting steel,
    Toes to frozen boot.

Stalked on into No Man's Land,
    Turned the wire to fleecy wool,
Iron stakes to sugar sticks
    Snapping at a pull.

Those who watched with hoary eyes
    Saw two figures gleaming there;
Hauptman Kälte, Colonel Cold,
    Gaunt, in the grey air.

Stiffly, tinkling spurs they moved
    Glassy eyed, with glinting heel
Stabbing those who lingered there
    Torn by screaming steel.

EDGELL RICKWOOD

The Leveller

Near Martinpuich that night of hell
Two men were struck by the same shell,
Together tumbling in one heap
Senseless and limp like slaughtered sheep.

One was a pale eighteen-year-old,
Blue-eyed and thin and not too bold,
Pressed for the war not ten years too soon,
The shame and pity of his platoon.

The other came from far-off lands
With bristling chin and whiskered hands,
He had known death and hell before
In Mexico and Ecuador.

Yet in his death this cut-throat wild
Groaned 'Mother! Mother!' like a child,
While that poor innocent in man's clothes
Died cursing God with brutal oaths.

Old Sergeant Smith, kindest of men,
Wrote out two copies there and then
Of his accustomed funeral speech
To cheer the womenfolk of each: –

'He died a hero's death: and we
His comrades of "A" Company
Deeply regret his death: we shall
All deeply miss so true a pal.'

ROBERT GRAVES

In Memoriam

Private D. Sutherland killed in action in the German trench, May 16th, 1916, and the others who died.

So you were David's father,
And he was your only son,
And the new-cut peats are rotting
And the work is left undone,
Because of an old man weeping,
Just an old man in pain,
For David, his son David,
That will not come again.

Oh, the letters he wrote you,
And I can see them still,
Not a word of the fighting
But just the sheep on the hill
And how you should get the crops in
Ere the year get stormier,
And the Bosches have got his body,
And I was his officer.

You were only David's father,
But I had fifty sons
When we went up in the evening
Under the arch of the guns,

And we came back at twilight –
O God! I heard them call
To me for help and pity
That could not help at all.

Oh, never will I forget you,
My men that trusted me,
More my sons than your fathers',
For they could only see
The little helpless babies
And the young men in their pride.
They could not see you dying,
And hold you while you died.

Happy and young and gallant,
They saw their first-born go,
But not the strong limbs broken
And the beautiful men brought low,
The piteous writhing bodies,
They screamed 'Don't leave me, sir,'
For they were only your fathers
But I was your officer.

E. A. MACKINTOSH

killed in action, 1916

To my Daughter Betty

In wiser days, my darling rosebud, blown
To beauty proud as was your Mother's prime.
In that desired, delayed, incredible time,
You'll ask why I abandoned you, my own,
And the dear heart that was your baby throne,

To dice with death. And oh! they'll give you rhyme
And reason: some will call the thing sublime,
And some decry it in a knowing tone.
So here, while the mad guns curse overhead,
And tired men sigh with mud for couch and floor,
Know that we fools, now with the foolish dead,
Died not for flag, nor King, nor Emperor,
But for a dream, born in a herdsman's shed,
And for the secret Scripture of the poor.

T. M. KETTLE
written four days before his death in action, 1916

Twelve Months After

Hullo! here's my platoon, the lot I had last year.
'The war'll be over soon.'
　　'What 'opes?'
　　　　'No bloody fear!'
Then, 'Number Seven, 'shun! All present and correct.'
They're standing in the sun, impassive and erect.
Young Gibson with his grin; and Morgan, tired and white;
Jordan, who's out to win a D.C.M. some night;
And Hughes that's keen on wiring; and Davies ('79),
Who always must be firing at the Boche front line.

*

'Old soldiers never die; they simply fide a-why!'
That's what they used to sing along the roads last spring;
That's what they used to say before the push began;
That's where they are today, knocked over to a man.

SIEGFRIED SASSOON

The General

'Good-morning; good-morning!' the General said
When we met him last week on our way to the line.
Now the soldiers he smiled at are most of 'em dead,
And we're cursing his staff for incompetent swine.
'He's a cheery old card,' grunted Harry to Jack
As they slogged up to Arras with rifle and pack.

*

But he did for them both by his plan of attack.

SIEGFRIED SASSOON

The Dug-out

Why do you lie with your legs ungainly huddled,
And one arm bent across your sullen, cold,
Exhausted face? It hurts my heart to watch you,
Deep-shadow'd from the candle's guttering gold;
And you wonder why I shake you by the shoulder;
Drowsy, you mumble and sigh and turn your head . . .
You are too young to fall asleep for ever;
And when you sleep you remind me of the dead.

SIEGFRIED SASSOON

To any Dead Officer

Well, how are things in Heaven? I wish you'd say,
    Because I'd like to know that you're all right.
Tell me, have you found everlasting day,
    Or been sucked in by everlasting night?

For when I shut my eyes your face shows plain;
    I hear you make some cheery old remark –
I can rebuild you in my brain,
    Though you've gone out patrolling in the dark.

You hated tours of trenches; you were proud
    Of nothing more than having good years to spend;
Longed to get home and join the careless crowd
    Of chaps who work in peace with Time for friend.
That's all washed out now. You're beyond the wire:
    No earthly chance can send you crawling back;
You've finished with machine-gun fire –
    Knocked over in a hopeless dud-attack.

Somehow I always thought you'd get done in,
    Because you were so desperate keen to live:
You were all out to try and save your skin,
    Well knowing how much the world had got to give.
You joked at shells and talked the usual 'shop',
    Stuck to your dirty job and did it fine:
With 'Jesus Christ! when *will* it stop?
    Three years . . . It's hell unless we break their line.'

So when they told me you'd been left for dead
    I wouldn't believe them, feeling it *must* be true.
Next week the bloody Roll of Honour said
    'Wounded and missing' – (That's the thing to do
When lads are left in shell-holes dying slow,
    With nothing but blank sky and wounds that ache,
Moaning for water till they know
    It's night, and then it's not worth while to wake!)

Good-bye, old lad! Remember me to God,
    And tell Him that our politicians swear
They won't give in till Prussian Rule's been trod
    Under the Heel of England . . . Are you there? . . .

Yes . . . and the War won't end for at least two years;
But we've got stacks of men . . . I'm blind with tears,
   Staring into the dark. Cheero!
I wish they'd killed you in a decent show.

SIEGFRIED SASSOON

Prelude: the Troops

Dim, gradual thinning of the shapeless gloom
Shudders to drizzling daybreak that reveals
Disconsolate men who stamp their sodden boots
And turn dulled, sunken faces to the sky
Haggard and hopeless. They, who have beaten down
The stale despair of night, must now renew
Their desolation in the truce of dawn,
Murdering the livid hours that grope for peace.

Yet these, who cling to life with stubborn hands,
Can grin through storms of death and find a gap
In the clawed, cruel tangles of his defence.
They march from safety, and the bird-sung joy
Of grass-green thickets, to the land where all
Is ruin, and nothing blossoms but the sky
That hastens over them where they endure
Sad, smoking, flat horizons, reeking woods,
And foundered trench-lines volleying doom for doom.

O my brave brown companions, when your souls
Flock silently away, and the eyeless dead
Shame the wild beast of battle on the ridge,
Death will stand grieving in that field of war
Since your unvanquished hardihood is spent.

And through some mooned Valhalla there will pass
Battalions and battalions, scarred from hell;
The unreturning army that was youth;
The legions who have suffered and are dust.

SIEGFRIED SASSOON

How Long, O Lord?

How long, O Lord, how long, before the flood
Of crimson-welling carnage shall abate?
From sodden plains in West and East the blood
Of kindly men streams up in mists of hate,
Polluting Thy clean air: and nations great
In reputation of the arts that bind
The world with hopes of Heaven, sink to the state
Of brute barbarians, whose ferocious mind
Gloats o'er the bloody havoc of their kind,
Not knowing love or mercy. Lord, how long
Shall Satan in high places lead the blind
To battle for the passions of the strong?
Oh, touch Thy children's hearts, that they may know
Hate their most hateful, pride their deadliest foe.

ROBERT PALMER
killed in action, 1916

Going into the Line

*At 3.15, No. 11 Platoon, 100 yards in rear of No. 10,
will move from Pommiers Redoubt.*

So soon!
At 3.15. And would return here . . . when?
It didn't say. Who would return? P'raps all,
P'raps none. Then it had come at last!

It had come at last! his own stupendous hour,
Long waited, dreaded, almost hoped-for too,
When all else seemed the foolery of power;
It had come at last! and suddenly the world
Was sharply cut in two. On one side lay
A golden, dreamy, peaceful afternoon,
And on the other, men gone mad with fear,
A hell of noise and darkness, a Last Day
Daily enacted. Now good-bye to one
And to the other . . . well, acceptance: that
At least he'd give; many had gone with joy:
He loathed it from his very inmost soul.

The golden world! It lay just over there,
Peacefully dreaming. In its clear bright depths
Friends moved – he saw them going here and there,
Like thistledown above an August meadow:
Gently as in a gentle dream they moved,
Unagonized, unwrought, nor sad, nor proud,
Faces he loved to agony – and none
Could see, or know, or bid him well-adieu.
Blasphemous irony! To think how oft
On such a day a friend would hold his hand
Saying good-bye, though they would meet next day,
And now . . . He breathed his whole soul out,
Bidding it span the unbridged senseless miles
And glow about their thoughts in waves of love.

'Twas time already! Now? As soon as this?
Did his voice hold? How did he look to them?
Poor craven little crowd of human mites!
Now they were crawling over the scarred cheese,
Silently going towards that roaring sea,
Each thinking his own thought, craving perhaps

A body that would fail, or with set teeth
Pitting a human will against the world.
Now every step seemed an eternity:
Each stretch of earth unreachable until it lay
Behind and a stretch longer lay beyond.
Would it never be ended? Crumbling earth,
Dry with the cracks of earthquake, dumbly showed
Death had just trodden there – and there he lay,
Foully deformed in what was once a man.
'Lo! as these are, so shalt thou be', he thought,
Shuddered: then thrilled almost to ecstasy,
As one from hell delivered up to heaven.

How slow they moved in front! Yes, slower still.
Then we must stop: we were not eighty yards.
But to stop here – to wait for it! Oh no!
Backward or forward, anything but not stop –
Not stand and wait! There's no alternative.
And now he rasps out, 'Halt!' They stand and curse,
Eyes furtive, fingers moving senselessly.
There comes a roar nearer and louder till
His head is bursting with noise and the earth shakes.
'A bloody near one, that!' and 'What the hell
Are we stuck here for?' come with sudden growls.
He moves without a word, and on they trudge.
So near! Yet nothing! Then how long? How long? . . .

And slowly in his overheated mind
Peace like a river through the desert flows,
And sweetness wells and overflows in streams
That reach the farthest friend in memory.
Peace now, and dear delight in serving these,
These poor sheep, driven innocent to death:
Peace undisturbed, though the poor senses jump,

And horror catches at the heart as when
Death unsuspected flaunts his grisly hand
Under the very eye of quietness:
Peace, peace with all, even the enemy,
Compassion for them deep as for his own:
Quietness now amid the thunderous noise,
And sweet elation in the grave of gloom.

MAX PLOWMAN
the Somme, August 1916

The Dead Soldiers

I

Spectrum Trench. Autumn. Nineteen-Sixteen.
And Zenith. (The Border Regiment will remember.)
A little north of where Lesboeufs had been.
(The Australians took it over in December.)
Just as the scythe had caught them, there they lay,
A sheaf for Death, ungarnered and untied:
A crescent moon of men who showed the way
When first the Tanks crept out, till they too died:
Guardsmen, I think, but one could hardly tell,
It was a forward slope, beyond the crest,
Muddier than any place in Dante's hell,
Where sniping gave us very little rest.
At night one stumbled over them and swore;
Each day the rain hid them a little more.

II

Fantastic forms, in posturing attitudes,
Twisted and bent, or lying deathly prone;
Their individual hopes my thought eludes,
But each man had a hope to call his own.

Much else? – God knows. But not for me the thought,
'Your mothers made your bodies: God your souls,
And, for because you dutifully fought,
God will go mad and make of half-lives, wholes.'
No. God in every one of you was slain;
For killing men is always killing God,
Though life destroyed shall come to life again
And loveliness rise from the sodden sod.
But if of life we do destroy the best,
God wanders wide, and weeps in his unrest.

MAX PLOWMAN

1917

Returning, we hear the Larks

Sombre the night is:
And, though we have our lives, we know
What sinister threat lurks there.

Dragging these anguished limbs, we only know
This poison-blasted track opens on our camp –
On a little safe sleep.

But hark! Joy – joy – strange joy.
Lo! Heights of night ringing with unseen larks:
Music showering on our upturned listening faces.

Death could drop from the dark
As easily as song –
But song only dropped,
Like a blind man's dreams on the sand
By dangerous tides;
Like a girl's dark hair, for she dreams no ruin lies there,
Or her kisses where a serpent hides.

ISAAC ROSENBERG

The Dying Soldier

'Here are houses,' he moaned,
'I could reach, but my brain swims.'
Then they thundered and flashed,
And shook the earth to its rims.

'They are gunpits,' he gasped,
'Our men are at the guns.
Water! . . . Water! . . . Oh, water!
For one of England's dying sons.'

'We cannot give you water,
Were all England in your breath.'
'Water! . . . Water! . . . Oh, water!'
He moaned and swooned to death.

ISAAC ROSENBERG

Break of Day in the Trenches

The darkness crumbles away –
It is the same old druid Time as ever.
Only a live thing leaps my hand –
A queer sardonic rat –
As I pull the parapet's poppy
To stick behind my ear.
Droll rat, they would shoot you if they knew
Your cosmopolitan sympathies
(And God knows what antipathies).
Now you have touched this English hand
You will do the same to a German –
Soon, no doubt, if it be your pleasure
To cross the sleeping green between.

It seems you inwardly grin as you pass
Strong eyes, fine limbs, haughty athletes
Less chanced than you for life,
Bonds to the whims of murder,
Sprawled in the bowels of the earth,
The torn fields of France.
What do you see in our eyes
At the shrieking iron and flame
Hurled through still heavens?
What quaver – what heart aghast?
Poppies whose roots are in man's veins
Drop, and are ever dropping;
But mine in my ear is safe,
Just a little white with the dust.

ISAAC ROSENBERG
killed in action, 1918

A Bitter Taste

*

Oh, see him in the House of Commons,
Passing laws to put down crime,
While the victims of his passions
Trudge on in mud and slime.

SONG

Sunsets

The white body of the evening
Is torn into scarlet,
Slashed and gouged and seared
Into crimson,
And hung ironically
With garlands of mist.

And the wind
Blowing over London from Flanders
Has a bitter taste.

RICHARD ALDINGTON

A Death-bed

'This is the State above the Law.
    The State exists for the State alone.'
(*This is a gland at the back of the jaw,
    And an answering lump by the collar-bone.*)

Some die shouting in gas or fire;
    Some die silent, by shell and shot.
Some die desperate, caught on the wire;
    Some die suddenly. This will not.

'Regis suprema voluntas Lex'
    (*It will follow the regular course of – throats.*)
Some die pinned by the broken decks,
    Some die sobbing between the boats.

Some die eloquent, pressed to death
    By the sliding trench, as their friends can hear.
Some die wholly in half a breath.
    Some – give trouble for half a year.

'There is neither Evil nor Good in life
    Except as the needs of the State ordain.'
(Since it is rather too late for the knife,
    All we can do is to mask the pain.)

Some die saintly in faith and hope –
    One died thus in a prison yard –
Some die broken by rape or the rope;
    Some die easily. This dies hard.

'I will dash to pieces who bar my way.
    Woe to the traitor! Woe to the weak!'
(Let him write what he wishes to say.
    It tires him out if he tries to speak.)

Some die quietly. Some abound
    In loud self-pity. Others spread
Bad morale through the cots around . . .
    This is a type that is better dead.

'The war was forced on me by my foes.
    All that I sought was the right to live.'
(Don't be afraid of a triple dose;
    The pain will neutralize half we give.

Here are the needles. See that he dies
    While the effects of the drug endure . . .
What is the question he asks with his eyes? –
    Yes, All-Highest, to God, be sure.)

RUDYARD KIPLING

Recruiting

'Lads, you're wanted, go and help,'
On the railway carriage wall
Stuck the poster, and I thought
Of the hands that penned the call.

Fat civilians wishing they
'Could go and fight the Hun.'
Can't you see them thanking God
That they're over forty-one?

Girls with feathers, vulgar songs –
Washy verse on England's need –
God – and don't we damned well know
How the message ought to read.

'Lads, you're wanted! over there,'
Shiver in the morning dew,
More poor devils like yourselves
Waiting to be killed by you.

Go and help to swell the names
In the casualty lists.
Help to make a column's stuff
For the blasted journalists.

Help to keep them nice and safe
From the wicked German foe.
Don't let him come over here!
'Lads, you're wanted – out you go.'

*

There's a better word than that,
Lads, and can't you hear it come
From a million men that call
You to share their martyrdom?

Leave the harlots still to sing
Comic songs about the Hun,
Leave the fat old men to say
Now *we've* got them on the run.

Better twenty honest years
Then their dull three score and ten.
Lads, you're wanted. Come and learn
To live and die with honest men.

You shall learn what men can do
If you will but pay the price,
Learn the gaiety and strength
In the gallant sacrifice.

Take your risk of life and death
Underneath the open sky.
Live clean or go out quick –
Lads, you're wanted. Come and die.

E. A. MACKINTOSH

Arm-chair

If I were now of handsome middle-age,
I should not govern yet, but still should hope
To help the prosecution of this war.
I'd talk and eat (though not eat wheaten bread),
I'd send my sons, if old enough, to France,
Or help to do my share in other ways.

All through the long spring evenings, when the sun
Pursued its primrose path toward the hills,
If fine, I'd plant potatoes on the lawn;
If wet, write anxious letters to the Press.
I'd give up wine and spirits, and with pride
Refuse to eat meat more than once a day,
And seek to rob the workers of their beer.
The only way to win a hard-fought war
Is to annoy the people in small ways,
Bully or patronize them, as you will!
I'd teach poor mothers, who have seven sons
– All fighting men of clean and sober life –
How to look after babies and to cook;
Teach them to save their money and invest;
Not to bring children up in luxury
– But do without a nursemaid in the house!

If I were old or only seventy,
Then should I be a great man in his prime.
I should rule army corps; at my command
Men would rise up, salute me, and attack
– And die. Or I might also govern men
By making speeches with my toothless jaws,
Constant in chatter, until men should say,
'One grand old man is still worth half his pay!'
That day, I'd send my grandsons out to France
– And wish I'd got ten other ones to send
(One cannot sacrifice too much, I'd say).
Then would I make a noble, toothless speech,
And all the list'ning Parliament would cheer.
'We cannot and we will not end this war
Till all the younger men with martial mien
Have enter'd capitals; never make peace
Till they are cripples, on one leg, or dead!'
Then would the Bishops go nigh mad with joy,

Cantuar, Ebor, and the other ones,
Be overwhelmed with pious ecstasy
In thanking Him we'd got a Christian,
An Englishman, still worth his salt, to talk.
In every pulpit would they preach and prance;
And our great Church would work, as heretofore,
To bring this poor old nation to its knees.
Then we'd forbid all liberty, and make
Free speech a relic of our impious past;
And when this war is finished, when the world
Is torn and bleeding, cut and bruised to death,
Then I'd pronounce my peace terms – to the poor!

But as it is, I am not ninety yet,
And so must pay my reverence to these men –
These grand old men, who still can see and talk,
Who sacrifice each other's sons each day.
O Lord! let me be ninety yet, I pray.
Methuselah was quite a youngster when
He died. Now, vainly weeping, we should say:
'Another great man perished in his prime!'
O let me govern, Lord, at ninety-nine!

                              OSBERT SITWELL

Base Details

If I were fierce, and bald, and short of breath,
    I'd live with scarlet Majors at the Base,
And speed glum heroes up the line to death.
    You'd see me with my puffy petulant face,
Guzzling and gulping in the best hotel,
    Reading the Roll of Honour. 'Poor young chap,'

I'd say – 'I used to know his father well;
   Yes, we've lost heavily in this last scrap.'
And when the war is done and youth stone dead,
I'd toddle safely home and die – in bed.

SIEGFRIED SASSOON

'Blighters'

The House is crammed: tier beyond tier they grin
And cackle at the Show, while prancing ranks
Of harlots shrill the chorus, drunk with din;
'We're sure the Kaiser loves our dear old Tanks!'

I'd like to see a Tank come down the stalls,
Lurching to rag-time tunes, or 'Home, sweet Home',
And there'd be no more jokes in Music-halls
To mock the riddled corpses round Bapaume.

SIEGFRIED SASSOON

Behind the Lines

*

Why did we join the army, boys?
Why did we join the army?
Why did we come to France to fight?
We must have been bloody well barmy.

SONG

Going up the Line

O consolation and refreshment breathed
From the young Spring with apple-blossom wreathed,
   Whose certain coming blesses
All life with token of immortality,
And from the ripe beauty and human tenderness
And reconcilement and tranquillity
Which are the spirit of all things grown old.
   For now that I have seen
The curd-white hawthorn once again
   Break out on the new green,
And through the iron gates in the long blank wall
   Have viewed across a screen
Of rosy apple-blossom the grey spire
And low red roofs and humble chimney-stacks,
And stood in spacious courtyards of old farms,
And heard green virgin wheat sing to the breeze,
And the drone of ancient worship rise and fall
In the dark church, and talked with simple folk
Of farm and village, dwelling near the earth,
Among earth's ancient, elemental things:
   I can with heart made bold
Go back into the ways of ruin and death
With step unflagging and with quiet breath,
For drawn from the hidden Spirit's deepest well
I carry in my soul a power to quell
   All ills and terrors such as these can hold.

MARTIN ARMSTRONG

Home Thoughts in Laventie

Green gardens in Laventie!
Soldiers only know the street
Where the mud is churned and splashed about
By battle-wending feet;
And yet beside one stricken house there is a glimpse of grass.
Look for it when you pass.

Beyond the church whose pitted spire
Seems balanced on a strand
Of swaying stone and tottering brick
Two roofless ruins stand,
And here behind the wreckage where the back wall should have been
We found a garden green.

The grass was never trodden on,
The little path of gravel
Was overgrown with celandine,
No other folk did travel
Along its weedy surface, but the nimble-footed mouse
Running from house to house.

So all among the vivid blades
Of soft and tender grass
We lay, nor heard the limber wheels
That pass and ever pass,
In noisy continuity until their very rattle
Seems in itself a battle.

At length we rose up from this ease
Of tranquil happy mind,
And searched the garden's little length
A fresh pleasaunce to find;
And there some yellow daffodils and jasmine hanging high
Did rest the tired eye.

The fairest and most fragrant
Of the many sweets we found,
Was a little bush of daphne flower
Upon a grassy mound,
And so thick were the blossoms set and so divine the scent
That we were well content.

Hungry for spring, I bent my head,
The perfume fanned my face,
And all my soul was dancing
In that lovely little place,
Dancing with a measured step from wrecked and shattered towns
Away upon the Downs.

I saw green banks of daffodil,
Slim poplars in the breeze,
Great tan-brown hares in gusty March
A-courting on the leas;
And meadows with their glittering streams, and silver scurrying
dace,
Home – what a perfect place!

E. W. TENNANT
killed in action, 1916

After the Battle

So they are satisfied with our Brigade,
And it remains to parcel out the bays!
And we shall have the usual Thanks Parade,
The beaming General, and the soapy praise.

You will come up in your capricious car
To find your heroes sulking in the rain,
To tell us how magnificent we are,
And how you hope we'll do the same again.

And we, who knew your old abusive tongue,
  Who heard you hector us a week before,
We who have bled to boost you up a rung –
  A K.C.B. perhaps, perhaps a Corps –

We who must mourn those spaces in the mess,
  And somehow fill those hollows in the heart,
We do not want your Sermon on Success,
  Your greasy benisons on Being Smart.

We only want to take our wounds away.
  To some warm village where the tumult ends,
And drowsing in the sunshine many a day,
  Forget our aches, forget that we had friends.

Weary we are of blood and noise and pain;
  This was a week we shall not soon forget;
And if, indeed, we have to fight again,
  We little wish to think about it yet.

We have done well; we like to hear it said.
  Say it, and then, for God's sake, say no more.
Fight, if you must, fresh battles far ahead,
  But keep them dark behind your chateau door!

                                        A. P. HERBERT

Beaucourt Revisited

I wandered up to Beaucourt; I took the river track,
And saw the lines we lived in before the Boche went back;
But Peace was now in Pottage, the front was far ahead,
The front had journeyed Eastward, and only left the dead.

And I thought, How long we lay there, and watched across the
    wire,
While the guns roared round the valley, and set the skies afire!
But now there are homes in Hamel and tents in the Vale of Hell,
And a camp at Suicide Corner, where half a regiment fell.

The new troops follow after, and tread the land we won,
To them 'tis so much hillside re-wrested from the Hun;
We only walk with reverence this sullen mile of mud;
The shell-holes hold our history, and half of them our blood.

Here, at the head of Peche Street, 'twas death to show your face;
To me it seemed like magic to linger in the place;
For me how many spirits hung round the Kentish Caves,
But the new men see no spirits – they only see the graves.

I found the half-dug ditches we fashioned for the fight
We lost a score of men there – young James was killed that night;
I saw the star-shells staring, I heard the bullets hail,
But the new troops pass unheeding – they never heard the tale.

I crossed the blood-red ribbon, that once was No Man's Land,
I saw a misty daybreak and a creeping minute-hand;
And here the lads went over, and there was Harmsworth shot,
And here was William lying – but the new men know them not.

And I said, 'There is still the river, and still the stiff, stark trees:
To treasure here our story, but there are only these';
But under the white wood crosses the dead men answered low,
'The new men know not Beaucourt, but we are here – we know.'

A. P. HERBERT

August, 1918

(In a French village)

I hear the tinkling of the cattle bell,
In the broad stillness of the afternoon;
High in the cloudless haze the harvest moon
Is pallid as the phantom of a shell.

A girl is drawing water from a well,
I hear the clatter of her wooden shoon;
Two mothers to their sleeping babies croon,
And the hot village feels the drowsy spell.

Sleep, child, the Angel of Death his wings has spread;
His engines scour the land, the sea, the sky;
And all the weapons of Hell's armoury

Are ready for the blood that is their bread;
And many a thousand men to-night must die,
So many that they will not count the Dead.

MAURICE BARING

Died of Wounds

His wet white face and miserable eyes
Brought nurses to him more than groans and sighs:
But hoarse and low and rapid rose and fell
His troubled voice: he did the business well.

The ward grew dark; but he was still complaining
And calling out for 'Dickie'. 'Curse the Wood!
It's time to go. O Christ, and what's the good?
We'll never take it, and it's always raining.'

I wondered where he'd been; then heard him shout,
'They snipe like hell! O Dickie, don't go out' . . .
I fell asleep . . . Next morning he was dead;
And some Slight Wound lay smiling on the bed.

SIEGFRIED SASSOON

Vlamertinghe

(Passing the Château, July 1917)

'And all her silken flanks with garlands drest' –
But we are coming to the sacrifice.
Must those have flowers who are not yet gone West?
May those have flowers who live with death and lice?

This must be the floweriest place
That earth allows; the queenly face
Of the proud mansion borrows grace for grace
Spite of those brute guns lowing at the skies.

Bold great daisies' golden lights,
Bubbling roses' pinks and whites –
Such a gay carpet! poppies by the million;
Such damask! such vermilion!
But if you ask me, mate, the choice of colour
Is scarcely right; this red should have been duller.

EDMUND BLUNDEN

Concert Party: Busseboom

The stage was set, the house was packed,
    The famous troop began;
Our laughter thundered, act by act;
    Time light as sunbeams ran.

Dance sprang and spun and neared and fled,
  Jest chirped at gayest pitch,
Rhythm dazzled, action sped
  Most comically rich.

With generals and lame privates both
  Such charms worked wonders, till
The show was over: lagging loth
  We faced the sunset chill;

And standing on the sandy way,
  With the cracked church peering past,
We heard another matinée,
  We heard the maniac blast

Of barrage south by Saint Eloi,
  And the red lights flaming there
Called madness: Come, my bonny boy,
  And dance to the latest air.

To this new concert, white we stood;
  Cold certainty held our breath;
While men in the tunnels below Larch Wood
  Were kicking men to death.

EDMUND BLUNDEN

O Jesus, Make it Stop

*

We're here because we're here
Because we're here, because we're here;
We're here because we're here
Because we're here, because we're here.

SONG

From *Gold Braid*

Same old trenches, same old view,
　　Same old rats as blooming tame,
Same old dug-outs, nothing new,
　　Same old smell, the very same,
Same old bodies out in front,
　　Same old *strafe* from two till four,
Same old scratching, same old 'unt,
　　Same old bloody war.

A. A. MILNE

Dead Cow Farm

An ancient saga tells us how
In the beginning the First Cow
(For nothing living yet had birth
But elemental cow on earth)
Began to lick cold stones and mud:
Under her warm tongue flesh and blood
Blossomed, a miracle to believe;
And so was Adam born, and Eve.
Here now is chaos once again,
Primaeval mud, cold stones and rain.
Here flesh decays and blood drips red,
And the Cow's dead, the old Cow's dead.

ROBERT GRAVES

The Rear-Guard

(Hindenburg Line, April 1917)

Groping along the tunnel, step by step,
He winked his prying torch with patching glare
From side to side, and sniffed the unwholesome air.

Tins, boxes, bottles, shapes too vague to know;
A mirror smashed, the mattress from a bed;
And he, exploring fifty feet below
The rosy gloom of battle overhead.

Tripping, he grabbed the wall; saw someone lie
Humped at his feet, half-hidden by a rug,
And stooped to give the sleeper's arm a tug.
'I'm looking for headquarters.' No reply.
'God blast your neck!' (For days he'd had no sleep,)
'Get up and guide me through this stinking place.'

Savage, he kicked a soft, unanswering heap,
And flashed his beam across the livid face
Terribly glaring up, whose eyes yet wore
Agony dying hard ten days before;
And fists of fingers clutched a blackening wound.

Alone he staggered on until he found
Dawn's ghost that filtered down a shafted stair
To the dazed, muttering creatures underground
Who hear the boom of shells in muffled sound.
At last, with sweat of horror in his hair,
He climbed through darkness to the twilight air,
Unloading hell behind him step by step.

SIEGFRIED SASSOON

Trench Duty

Shaken from sleep, and numbed and scarce awake,
Out in the trench with three hours' watch to take,
I blunder through the splashing mirk; and then
Hear the gruff muttering voices of the men
Crouching in cabins candle-chinked with light.

Hark! There's the big bombardment on our right
Rumbling and bumping; and the dark's a glare
Of flickering horror in the sectors where
We raid the Boche; men waiting, stiff and chilled,
Or crawling on their bellies through the wire.
'What? Stretcher-bearers wanted? Someone killed?'
Five minutes ago I heard a sniper fire:
Why did he do it? . . . Starlight overhead –
Blank stars. I'm wide-awake; and some chap's dead.

SIEGFRIED SASSOON

The Mad Soldier

I dropp'd here three weeks ago, yes – I know,
And it's bitter cold at night, since the fight –
I could tell you if I chose – no one knows
Excep' me and four or five, what ain't alive.
I can see them all asleep, three men deep,
And they're nowhere near a fire – but our wire
Has 'em fast as can be. Can't you see
When the flare goes up? Ssh! boys; what's that noise?
Do you know what these rats eat? Body-meat!
After you've been down a week, an' your cheek
Gets as pale as life, and night seems as white
As the day, only the rats and their brats
Seem more hungry when the day's gone away –
An' they look as big as bulls, an' they pulls
Till you almost sort o' shout – but the drought
What you hadn't felt before makes you sore.
And at times you even think of a drink . . .
There's a leg across my thighs – if my eyes
Weren't too sore, I'd like to see who it be,
Wonder if I'd know the bloke if I woke? –
Woke? By damn, I'm not asleep – there's a heap

Of us wond'ring why the hell we're not well . . .
Leastways I am – since I came it's the same
With the others – they don't know what *I* do,
Or they wouldn't gape and grin. – It's a sin
To say that Hell is hot – 'cause it's not:
Mind you, I know very well we're in hell. –
In a twisted hump we lie – heaping high,
Yes! an' higher every day. – Oh, I say,
This chap's heavy on my thighs – damn his eyes.

E. W. TENNANT
1916

Louse Hunting

Nudes, stark and glistening,
Yelling in lurid glee. Grinning faces
And raging limbs
Whirl over the floor on fire;
For a shirt verminously busy
Yon soldier tore from his throat
With oaths
Godhead might shrink at, but not the lice,
And soon the shirt was aflare
Over the candle he'd lit while we lay.

Then we all sprang up and stript
To hunt the verminous brood.
Soon like a demons' pantomime
This plunge was raging.
See the silhouettes agape,
See the gibbering shadows
Mixed with the baffled arms on the wall.
See gargantuan hooked fingers
Pluck in supreme flesh
To smutch supreme littleness.

See the merry limbs in that Highland fling
Because some wizard vermin willed
To charm from the quiet this revel
When our ears were half lulled
By the dark music
Blown from Sleep's trumpet.

ISAAC ROSENBERG

Dead Man's Dump

The plunging limbers over the shattered track
Racketed with their rusty freight,
Stuck out like many crowns of thorns,
And the rusty stakes like sceptres sold
To stay the flood of brutish men
Upon our brothers dear.

The wheels lurched over sprawled dead
But pained them not, though their bones crunched;
Their shut mouths made no moan.
They lie there huddled, friend and foeman,
Man born of man, and born of woman;
And shells go crying over them
From night till night and now.

Earth has waited for them
All the time of their growth
Fretting for their decay:
Now she has them at last!
In the strength of their strength
Suspended – stopped and held.

What fierce imaginings their dark souls lit?
Earth! Have they gone into you?
Somewhere they must have gone,
And flung on your hard back
Is their souls' sack,
Emptied of God-ancestralled essences.
Who hurled them out? Who hurled?

None saw their spirits' shadow shake the grass,
Or stood aside for the half used life to pass
Out of those doomed nostrils and the doomed mouth,
When the swift iron burning bee
Drained the wild honey of their youth.

What of us who, flung on the shrieking pyre,
Walk, our usual thoughts untouched,
Our lucky limbs as on ichor fed,
Immortal seeming ever?
Perhaps when the flames beat loud on us,
A fear may choke in our veins
And the startled blood may stop.
The air is loud with death,
The dark air spurts with fire,
The explosions ceaseless are.
Timelessly now, some minutes past,
These dead strode time with vigorous life,
Till the shrapnel called 'An end!'
But not to all. In bleeding pangs
Some borne on stretchers dreamed of home,
Dear things, war-blotted from their hearts.

A man's brains splattered on
A stretcher-bearer's face:
His shook shoulders slipped their load,

But when they bent to look again
The drowning soul was sunk too deep
For human tenderness.

They left this dead with the older dead,
Stretched at the cross roads.

Burnt black by strange decay
Their sinister faces lie,
The lid over each eye;
The grass and coloured clay
More motion have than they,
Joined to the great sunk silences.

Here is one not long dead.
His dark hearing caught our far wheels,
And the choked soul stretched weak hands
To reach the living world the far wheels said;
The blood-dazed intelligence beating for light,
Crying through the suspense of the far-torturing wheels
Swift for the end to break
Or the wheels to break,
Cried as the tick of the world broke over his sight,
'Will they come? Will they ever come?'
Even as the mixed hoofs of the mules,
The quivering-bellied mules,
And the rushing wheels all mixed
With his tortured upturned sight.

So we crashed round the bend,
We heard his weak scream,
We heard his very last sound,
And our wheels grazed his dead face.

ISAAC ROSENBERG

From *In Parenthesis:* Part 7

The First Field Dressing is futile as frantic as seaman's shift
bunged to stoved bulwark, so soon the darking flood percolates
and he dies in your arms.
  And get back to that digging can't yer –
this ain't a bloody Wake
        for these dead, who will soon have their dead
for burial clods heaped over.
Nor time for halsing
nor to clip green wounds
nor weeping Maries bringing anointments
neither any word spoken
nor no decent nor appropriate sowing of this seed
nor remembrance of the harvesting
of the renascent cycle
and return
nor shaving of the head nor ritual incising for these *viriles*
    under each tree
  No one sings: Lully lully
for the mate whose blood runs down.

DAVID JONES

Anthem for Doomed Youth

What passing bells for those who die as cattle?
  Only the monstrous anger of the guns.
  Only the stuttering rifles' rapid rattle
Can patter out their hasty orisons.
No mockeries for them from prayers or bells,
  Nor any voice of mourning save the choirs, –
The shrill, demented choirs of wailing shells;
  And bugles calling for them from sad shires.

What candles may be held to speed them all?
Not in the hands of boys, but in their eyes
Shall shine the holy glimmers of good-byes.
The pallor of girls' brows shall be their pall;
Their flowers the tenderness of patient minds,
And each slow dusk a drawing-down of blinds.

WILFRED OWEN

Exposure

Our brains ache, in the merciless iced east winds that knive us . . .
Wearied we keep awake because the night is silent . . .
Low, drooping flares confuse our memories of the salient . . .
Worried by silence, sentries whisper, curious, nervous,
    But nothing happens.

Watching, we hear the mad gusts tugging on the wire,
Like twitching agonies of men among its brambles.
Northward, incessantly, the flickering gunnery rumbles,
Far off, like a dull rumour of some other war.
    What are we doing here?

The poignant misery of dawn begins to grow . . .
We only know war lasts, rain soaks, and clouds sag stormy.
Dawn massing in the east her melancholy army
Attacks once more in ranks on shivering ranks of grey,
    But nothing happens.

Sudden successive flights of bullets streak the silence.
Less deadly than the air that shudders black with snow,
With sidelong flowing flakes that flock, pause, and renew,
We watch them wandering up and down the wind's nonchalance,
    But nothing happens.

Pale flakes with fingering stealth come feeling for our faces –
We cringe in holes, back on forgotten dreams, and stare, snow-
    dazed,
Deep into grassier ditches. So we drowse, sun-dozed,
Littered with blossoms trickling where the blackbird fusses.
    Is it that we are dying?

Slowly our ghosts drag home: glimpsing the sunk fires, glozed
With crusted dark-red jewels; crickets jingle there;
For hours the innocent mice rejoice: The house is theirs;
Shutters and doors, all closed: on us the doors are closed, –
    We turn back to our dying.

Since we believe not otherwise can kind fires burn;
Nor ever suns smile true on child, or field, or fruit.
For God's invincible spring our love is made afraid;
Therefore, not loath, we lie out here; therefore were born,
    For love of God seems dying.

Tonight, His frost will fasten on this mud and us,
Shrivelling many hands, puckering foreheads crisp.
The burying party, picks and shovels in the shaking grasp,
Pause over half-known faces. All their eyes are ice,
    But nothing happens.

                  WILFRED OWEN

The Sentry

We'd found an old Boche dug-out, and he knew,
And gave us hell, for shell on frantic shell
Hammered on top, but never quite burst through.
Rain, guttering down in waterfalls of slime,

Kept slush waist high that, rising hour by hour,
Choked up the steps too thick with clay to climb.
What murk of air remained stank old, and sour
With fumes of whizz-bangs, and the smell of men
Who'd lived there years, and left their curse in the den,
If not their corpses . . .
                         There we herded from the blast
Of whizz-bangs, but one found our door at last.
Buffeting eyes and breath, snuffing the candles,
And thud! flump! thud! down the steep steps came thumping
And sploshing in the flood, deluging muck –
The sentry's body; then his rifle, handles
Of old Boche bombs, and mud in ruck on ruck.
We dredged him up, for killed, until he whined
'O sir, my eyes – I'm blind – I'm blind, I'm blind!'
Coaxing, I held a flame against his lids
And said if he could see the least blurred light
He was not blind; in time he'd get all right.
'I can't,' he sobbed. Eyeballs, huge-bulged like squids',
Watch my dreams still; but I forgot him there
In posting next for duty, and sending a scout
To beg a stretcher somewhere, and floundering about
To other posts under the shrieking air.

Those other wretches, how they bled and spewed,
And one who would have drowned himself for good, –
I try not to remember these things now.
Let dread hark back for one word only: how
Half-listening to that sentry's moans and jumps,
And the wild chattering of his broken teeth,
Renewed most horribly whenever crumps
Pummelled the roof and slogged the air beneath –
Through the dense din, I say, we heard him shout
'I see your lights!' But ours had long died out.
                                        WILFRED OWEN

Strange Meeting

It seemed that out of battle I escaped
Down some profound dull tunnel, long since scooped
Through granites which titanic wars had groined.
Yet also there encumbered sleepers groaned,
Too fast in thought or death to be bestirred.
Then, as I probed them, one sprang up, and stared
With piteous recognition in fixed eyes,
Lifting distressful hands as if to bless.
And by his smile, I knew that sullen hall,
By his dead smile I knew we stood in Hell.
With a thousand pains that vision's face was grained;
Yet no blood reached there from the upper ground,
And no guns thumped, or down the flues made moan.
'Strange friend', I said, 'here is no cause to mourn.'
'None,' said the other, 'save the undone years,
The hopelessness. Whatever hope is yours,
Was my life also; I went hunting wild
After the wildest beauty in the world,
Which lies not calm in eyes, or braided hair,
But mocks the steady running of the hour,
And if it grieves, grieves richlier than here.
For of my glee might many men have laughed,
And of my weeping something had been left,
Which must die now. I mean the truth untold,
The pity of war, the pity war distilled.
Now men will go content with what we spoiled.
Or, discontent, boil bloody, and be spilled.
They will be swift with swiftness of the tigress,
None will break ranks, though nations trek from progress.
Courage was mine, and I had mystery,
Wisdom was mine, and I had mastery;

To miss the march of this retreating world
Into vain citadels that are not walled.
Then, when much blood had clogged their chariot-wheels,
I would go up and wash them from sweet wells,
Even with truths that lie too deep for taint.
I would have poured my spirit without stint
But not through wounds; not on the cess of war.
Foreheads of men have bled where no wounds were.
I am the enemy you killed, my friend.
I knew you in this dark: for so you frowned
Yesterday through me as you jabbed and killed.
I parried; but my hands were loath and cold.
Let us sleep now . . .'

WILFRED OWEN
found among his papers

Dulce et Decorum est

Bent double, like old beggars under sacks,
Knock-kneed, coughing like hags, we cursed through sludge,
Till on the haunting flares we turned our backs,
And towards our distant rest began to trudge.
Men marched asleep. Many had lost their boots,
But limped on, blood-shod. All went lame, all blind;
Drunk with fatigue; deaf even to the hoots
Of gas-shells dropping softly behind.

Gas! Gas! Quick, boys! – An ecstasy of fumbling,
Fitting the clumsy helmets just in time,
But someone still was yelling out and stumbling
And floundering like a man in fire or lime. –
Dim through the misty panes and thick green light,
As under a green sea, I saw him drowning.

In all my dreams, before my helpless sight,
He plunges at me, guttering, choking, drowning.

If in some smothering dreams, you too could pace
Behind the wagon that we flung him in,
And watch the white eyes writhing in his face,
His hanging face, like a devil's sick of sin;
If you could hear, at every jolt, the blood
Come gargling from the froth-corrupted lungs,
Obscene as cancer, bitter as the cud
Of vile, incurable sores on innocent tongues, –
My friend, you would not tell with such high zest
To children ardent for some desperate glory,
The old Lie: Dulce et decorum est
Pro patria mori.

WILFRED OWEN

killed in action, 1918

Attack

At dawn the ridge emerges massed and dun
In the wild purple of the glow'ring sun,
Smouldering through spouts of drifting smoke that shroud
The menacing scarred slope; and, one by one,
Tanks creep and topple forward to the wire.
The barrage roars and lifts. Then, clumsily bowed
With bombs and guns and shovels and battle-gear,
Men jostle and climb to meet the bristling fire.
Lines of grey, muttering faces, masked with fear,
They leave their trenches, going over the top,
While time ticks blank and busy on their wrists,
And hope, with furtive eyes and grappling fists,
Flounders in mud. O Jesus, make it stop!

SIEGFRIED SASSOON

At Last, at Last!

*

Après la guerre fini
Tous les soldats partis,
Mademoiselle avec piccaninni,
Souvenir des Anglais.

SONG

Bacchanal

Into the twilight of Trafalgar Square
They pour from every quarter, banging drums
And tootling penny trumpets – to a blare
Of tin mouth-organs, while a sailor strums
A solitary banjo, lads and girls
Locked in embraces in a wild dishevel
Of flags and streaming hair, with curdling skirls
Surge in a frenzied reeling panic revel.

Lads who so long have stared death in the face,
Girls who so long have tended death's machines,
Released from the numb terror shriek and prance –
And, watching them, I see the outrageous dance,
The frantic torches and the tambourines
Tumultuous on the midnight hills of Thrace.

WILFRID GIBSON
November, 1918

A Dirge of Victory

Lift not thy trumpet, Victory, to the sky,
   Nor through battalions nor by batteries blow,
   But over hollows full of old wire go,
Where, among dregs of war, the long-dead lie
With wasted iron that the guns passed by
   When they went eastward like a tide at flow;
   There blow thy trumpet that the dead may know,
Who waited for thy coming, Victory.

It is not we that have deserved thy wreath.
　They waited there among the towering weeds:
The deep mud burned under the thermite's breath,
　And winter cracked the bones that no man heeds:
Hundreds of nights flamed by: the seasons passed.
And thou hast come to them at last, at last!

LORD DUNSANY

Now to be Still and Rest

Now to be still and rest, while the heart remembers
　All that it learned and loved in the days long past,
To stoop and warm our hands at the fallen embers,
　Glad to have come to the long way's end at last.

Now to awake, and feel no regret at waking,
　Knowing the shadowy days are white again,
To draw our curtains and watch the slow dawn breaking
　Silver and grey on English field and lane.

Now to fulfil our dreams, in woods and meadows
　Treading the well-loved paths – to pause and cry
'So, even so I remember it' – seeing the shadows
　Weave on the distant hills their tapestry.

Now to rejoice in children and join their laughter,
　Tuning our hearts once more to the fairy strain,
To hear our names on voices we love, and after
　Turn with a smile to sleep and our dreams again.

Then – with a new-born strength, the sweet rest over,
    Gladly to follow the great white road once more,
To work with a song on our lips and the heart of a lover,
    Building a city of peace on the wastes of war.

P. H. B. LYON

Back

They ask me where I've been,
And what I've done and seen.
But what can I reply
Who know it wasn't I,
But someone just like me,
Who went across the sea
And with my head and hands
Killed men in foreign lands . . .
Though I must bear the blame,
Because he bore my name.

WILFRID GIBSON

Envoi

How shall I say goodbye to you, wonderful, terrible days,
If I should live to live and leave 'neath an alien soil
You, my men, who taught me to walk with a smile in the ways
Of the valley of shadows, taught me to know you and love you,
    and toil
Glad in the glory of fellowship, happy in misery, strong
In the strength that laughs at its weakness, laughs at its sorrows
    and fears,
Facing the world that was not too kind with a jest and a song?
What can the world hold afterwards worthy of laughter or tears?

EDWARD DE STEIN

Two Fusiliers

And have we done with War at last?
Well, we've been lucky devils both,
And there's no need of pledge or oath
To bind our lovely friendship fast,
By firmer stuff
Close bound enough.

By wire and wood and stake we're bound,
By Fricourt and Festubert,
By whipping rain, by the sun's glare,
By all the misery and loud sound,
By a Spring day,
By Picard clay.

Show me the two so closely bound
As we, by the wet bond of blood,
By friendship blossoming from mud,
By Death: we faced him, and we found
Beauty in Death,
In dead men, breath.

ROBERT GRAVES

A Dead Statesman

I could not dig: I dared not rob:
Therefore I lied to please the mob.
Now all my lies are proved untrue
And I must face the men I slew.
What tale shall serve me here among
Mine angry and defrauded young?

RUDYARD KIPLING

This Generation

Their youth was fevered – passionate, quick to drain
   The last few pleasures from the cup of life
Before they turned to suck the dregs of pain
   And end their young-old lives in mortal strife.
They paid the debts of many a hundred year
   Of foolishness and riches in alloy.
They went to death; nor did they shed a tear
   For all they sacrificed of love and joy.
Their tears ran dry when they were in the womb,
For, entering life – they found it was their tomb.

OSBERT SITWELL

Here Dead we Lie

Here dead we lie because we did not choose
   To live and shame the land from which we sprung.
Life, to be sure, is nothing much to lose;
   But young men think it is, and we were young.

A. E. HOUSMAN

From *How Shall we Rise to Greet the Dawn?*

Continually they cackle thus,
These venerable birds,
Crying, 'Those whom the Gods love
Die young'
Or something of that sort.

OSBERT SITWELL

Common Form

If any question why we died,
Tell them, because our fathers lied.

RUDYARD KIPLING

The Watchers

I heard the Challenge 'Who goes there?'
Close-kept but mine through midnight air;
I answered and was recognized,
And passed, and kindly thus advised:
'There's someone crawlin' through the grass
By the red ruin, or there was,
And them machine-guns been a firin'
All the time the chaps was wirin',
So sir if you're goin' out
You'll keep your 'ead well down no doubt.'

When will the stern fine 'Who goes there?'
Meet me again in midnight air?
And the gruff sentry's kindness, when
Will kindness have such power again?
It seems, as now I wake and brood,
And know my hour's decrepitude,
That on some dewy parapet
The sentry's spirit gazes yet,
Who will not speak with altered tone
When I at last am seen and known.

EDMUND BLUNDEN

Envoi

... my song no answer brings
nor in the calm a whisper stirs
the leaves, no dawn to me
but waking-time and I bereft
betrayed their trust
     for others move
to follow them
   This not the song they wish to hear.

But men have died to give them place
and they who live will one day sing
as I, will speak their sorrow once again,
but some will hear with sound a song
to lead the children into love
     Whose children these?
     Not theirs who died.

O Mercy give us grace to live
O God send wisdom soon.

       WYN GRIFFITH
     from The Song is Theirs

A Short Poem for Armistice Day

Gather or take fierce degree
trim the lamp set out for sea
here we are at the workman's entrance
clock in and shed your eminence.

Notwithstanding, work it diverse ways
work it diverse days, multiplying four digestions
here we make artificial flowers
of paper tin and metal thread.

One eye one leg one arm one lung
a syncopated sick heart-beat
the record is not nearly worn
that weaves a background to our work.

I have no power therefore have patience
These flowers have no sweet scent
no lustre in the petal no increase
from fertilizing flies and bees.

No seed they have no seed
their tendrils are of wire and grip
the buttonhole the lip
and never fade

And will not fade though life
and lustre go in genuine flowers
and men like flowers are cut
and withered on a stem.
And will not fade a year or more
I stuck one in a candlestick
and there it clings about the socket
I have no power therefore have patience.

HERBERT READ

To One Who Was With Me in the War

It was too long ago – that Company which we served with . . .
We call it back in visual fragments, you and I,
Who seem, ourselves, like relics casually preserved with

Our mindfulness of old bombardments when the sky
With blundering din blinked cavernous.
                                Yet a sense of power
Invades us when, recapturing an ungodly hour
Of ante-zero crisis, in one thought we've met
To stand in some redoubt of Time, – to share again
All but the actual wetness of the flare-lit rain,
All but the living presences who haunt us yet
With gloom-patrolling eyes.
                        Remembering, we forget
Much that was monstrous, much that clogged our souls with clay
When hours were guides who led us by the longest way –
And when the worst had been endured could still disclose
Another worst to thwart us . . .
                        We forget our fear . . .
And, while the uncouth Event begins to lour less near,
Discern the mad magnificence whose storm-light throws
Wild shadows on these after-thoughts that send your brain
Back beyond Peace, exploring sunken ruinous roads.
Your brain, with files of flitting forms hump-backed with loads,
On its own helmet hears the tinkling drops of rain, –
Follows to an end some night-relief, and strangely sees
The quiet no-man's-land of daybreak, jagg'd with trees
That loom like giant Germans . . .
                        I'll go with you, then,
Since you must play this game of ghosts. At listening-posts
We'll peer across dim craters; joke with jaded men
Whose names we've long forgotten. (Stoop low there; it's the place
The sniper enfilades.) Round the next bay you'll meet
A drenched platoon-commander; chilled, he drums his feet
On squelching duck-boards; winds his wrist-watch; turns his head,
And shows you how you looked, – your ten-years-vanished face,
Hoping the War will end next week . . .
                        What's that you said?
                                SIEGFRIED SASSOON

Aftermath

Have you forgotten yet? . . .
For the world's events have rumbled on since those gagged days,
Like traffic checked while at the crossing of city-ways:
And the haunted gap in your mind has filled with thoughts that flow
Like clouds in the lit heaven of life; and you're a man reprieved
    to go,
Taking your peaceful share of Time, with joy to spare.
But the past is just the same – and War's a bloody game . . .
Have you forgotten yet? . . .
Look down, and swear by the slain of the War that you'll never forget.

Do you remember the dark months you held the sector at Mametz –
The nights you watched and wired and dug and piled sandbags on
    parapets?
Do you remember the rats; and the stench
Of corpses rotting in front of the front-line trench –
And dawn coming, dirty-white, and chill with a hopeless rain?
Do you ever stop and ask, 'Is it all going to happen again?'

Do you remember that hour of din before the attack –
And the anger, the blind compassion that seized and shook you then
As you peered at the doomed and haggard faces of your men?
Do you remember the stretcher-cases lurching back
With dying eyes and lolling heads – those ashen-grey
Masks of the lads who once were keen and kind and gay?

Have you forgotten yet? . . .
Look up, and swear by the green of the spring that you'll never forget.

SIEGFRIED SASSOON

March 1919

Epilogue

High Wood

Ladies and gentlemen, this is High Wood,
Called by the French, Bois des Fourneaux,
The famous spot which in Nineteen-Sixteen,
July, August and September was the scene
Of long and bitterly contested strife,
By reason of its High commanding site.
Observe the effect of shell-fire in the trees
Standing and fallen; here is wire; this trench
For months inhabited, twelve times changed hands;
(They soon fall in), used later as a grave.
It has been said on good authority
That in the fighting for this patch of wood
Were killed somewhere above eight thousand men,
Of whom the greater part were buried here,
This mound on which you stand being . . .

> Madame, please,

You are requested kindly not to touch
Or take away the Company's property
As souvenirs; you'll find we have on sale
A large variety, all guaranteed.
As I was saying, all is as it was,
This is an unknown British officer,
The tunic having lately rotted off.
Please follow me – this way . . .

> the *path*, sir, *please*,

The ground which was secured at great expense
The Company keeps absolutely untouched,
And in that dug-out (genuine) we provide
Refreshments at a reasonable rate.
You are requested not to leave about
Paper, or ginger-beer bottles, or orange-peel,
There are waste-paper baskets at the gate.

PHILIP JOHNSTONE
1918

Biographies

Biographies

* Died on Active Service

RICHARD ALDINGTON. Born in 1892, and educated at Dover College and London University. He served on the Western Front, 1916–18; was badly gassed, the after-effects of which never left him. After the War he wrote the famous, indignant war book *Death of a Hero*. Novelist, poet, and controversial biographer, he died at his home in the South of France in 1962. *Collected Poems* (Allen & Unwin, 1929). Aldington was a leading exponent of the Imagist school of poetry, which derived from the ideas of *T. E. HULME, critic and philosopher, who was also friendly with Wilfrid Gibson. Hulme served in the R.A., and was wounded in France – which provoked another Imagist, EZRA POUND, to write in Canto XVI:

> And old T.E.H. he went to it,
> With a lot of books from the library,
> London Library, and a shell buried 'em in a dug-out,
> And the Library expressed its annoyance.
> And a bullet hit him in the elbow
> . . . gone through the fellow in front of him,
> And he read Kant in hospital, in Wimbledon, in the original,
> And the hospital staff didn't like it.

Hulme returned to the Front, where he was killed by German shell-fire near Nieuport, 1917.

MARTIN ARMSTRONG. Born in Newcastle-on-Tyne, 1882, and educated at Charterhouse and Pembroke College, Cambridge. First collection of poems published in 1912. He served in the ranks in the 2nd Artist's Rifles, 1914–15; commissioned in 8th Middlesex

Regt., 1915–19. Served in France on the Western Front. *The Buzzards and Other Poems* (Secker, 1921). Author.

HERBERT ASQUITH. Son of H. H. Asquith, Prime Minister 1908–16, he was born in 1881, and educated at Winchester and Balliol College, Oxford. President of the Oxford Union; Called to the Bar, 1907. He mixed with the Georgian poets before the War, and was a friend of D. H. Lawrence. Captain, R.A.; Western Front. *The Volunteer and Other Poems* (Sidgwick & Jackson); *Poems 1912–33* (Sidgwick & Jackson, 1934). He died in 1947. He was the brother of Arthur Asquith (q.v. Rupert Brooke), and
*RAYMOND ASQUITH, who was also educated at Winchester and Balliol, also President of the Union, and also Called to the Bar. Raymond Asquith has often been written of as the most brilliant man of his generation. At Oxford he was awarded Craven, Derby, Ireland, and Eldon scholarships, and was a Fellow of All Souls. British delegate at a fisheries dispute, at The Hague, 1911. Lieutenant in the Grenadier Guards; killed at the Battle of the Somme, 1916. He wrote some light verse. A. A. Milne said in 1954: 'I thought then, and have never ceased to think, the most brilliant man I have ever met'. For the young Asquiths see *Edward Marsh*, by Christopher Hassall (Longmans, 1959).

MAURICE BARING. Born in 1874, the fourth son of Lord Revelstoke, and educated at Eton and Trinity College, Cambridge. A friend of Marsh, he joined the diplomatic service, and then became a foreign correspondent for *The Morning Post* and *The Times*. Intelligence Corps, 1914; attached to R.F.C., and later with R.A.F. Personal Secretary to General Sir H. Trenchard, 1918. Man of letters after the War. *Collected Poems* (Heinemann, 1925). He died in 1945.

LEONARD BARNES. *Youth at Arms* (Peter Davies, 1933).

PAUL BEWSHER. Born in 1894, and educated at St Paul's. A journalist before the war, he joined the Royal Naval Air Service, and became a captain. He was shot down in the sea, wounded, and awarded the D.S.C. At one time his task was to bomb towns behind the lines, and he wrote many poems on his doubts and self-torments on these assignments. They were published in various magazines, and mostly collected in *The Bombing of Bruges* (Hodder & Stoughton, 1918). He also published another collection and an autobiographical account of his experiences. After the war he worked for the *Daily Mail* for many years.

LAURENCE BINYON. Born in 1869, and educated at St Paul's and Trinity College, Oxford. In charge of a sub-department of oriental prints and drawings at the British Museum, he visited the Front in 1916 as a Red Cross orderly. Binyon, a melancholy poet, found much inspiration from the War; he was overwhelmed by the decimation of the younger generation. *For the Fallen* (which first appeared in *The Times*, September 21, 1914, and not, as is so often thought, at the end of the war) is quoted on countless memorials. Binyon spent 40 years at the Museum, and died in 1943, after a time as Professor of Poetry at Harvard. *The Four Years* (Elkin Mathews, 1919).

EDMUND BLUNDEN. Born in 1896, and educated at Christ's Hospital, where he began writing poetry, and at Queen's College, Oxford. He served with The Royal Sussex Regiment, 1915–19, fought at the Somme and Ypres, and won the Military Cross. Author of the great war book *Undertones of War* (Oxford University Press edition, 1956, contains thirty-two of his best war poems). It was written while he was teaching English at Tokyo University (Robert Nichols held the post before him). He was awarded the Hawthornden Prize in 1922. Fellow of Merton College, Oxford, 1931–44. Professor of English Literature, University of Hong Kong. Great and long-standing friend of Siegfried Sassoon. C.B.E., 1951.

JOHN PEALE BISHOP. Born in Charles Town, Virginia, in 1892, and educated at Princeton. He served in France with U.S. 33rd Infantry. After the war, editor, man of letters, and Francophile; life-long friend of Edmund Wilson and Scott Fitzgerald (who admired Rupert Brooke). Died: 1944. *Selected Poems* (Chatto & Windus, 1960). Other American poets who served in U.S. Army during the war were MARK VAN DOREN, EDMUND WILSON and ARCHIBALD MACLEISH (his *Memorial Rain* is one of the best-known American war poems). WILLIAM FAULKNER, who served in the R.F.C., also wrote war poetry, but none of it has survived. Faulkner went to France, after training in Canada, but crashed a plane and was injured; he was not shot down in action as legend sometimes has it. He was made an 'Honorary' second lieutenant on December 22, 1918, the date of demobilization, and relinquished his commission the following day. His first novel, *Soldier's Pay*, told of the bitter homecoming of a dying soldier. He was deeply influenced by what he had seen of the war, and what he had heard of it from the disillusioned young men he had met. His bleak war stories are among the finest literature to have come out of the holocaust: stories like *Ad Astra*, *Victory*, and *Crevasse*.

*RUPERT BROOKE. Born in 1887, and educated at Rugby (his father was a master there), and at King's College, Cambridge, where he was a close friend of Hugh Dalton and joined the Fabians. Influenced by F. H. Keeling, one of the leading Fabians of the day (killed at the Somme in 1916). A brilliant undergraduate career; made a Fellow of his college. Travelled widely around the world before the war. Sent to Canada and the United States by the *Westminster Gazette* to write a series of articles. His poems had a tremendous impact on his slightly younger contemporaries, such as W. N. Hodgson; a first collection was published in 1911. Suffused with patriotism, he was happy, almost anxious, to die for his country in battle. A friend of Masefield, Gibson, Abercrombie, Drinkwater, and the young Asquiths (he sometimes stayed at 10 Downing

Street when on leave). Given a commission (sub-lieutenant) in the Royal Naval Division by Winston Churchill (First Lord of the Admiralty). Saw some action at Antwerp in 1914. Died on St George's Day, 1915, on the way to Gallipoli, not in battle but of acute blood poisoning. He was buried on the Greek island of Scyros, associated with Achilles. He was surrounded by his friends, including Arthur Asquith (the Prime Minister's third son, who was a brigadier-general by 1918 at the age of 35 – the second youngest in the Army – with a D.S.O. and two bars), Bernard Freyberg, V.C. (later Governor-General of New Zealand), Patrick Shaw-Stewart (q.v.), and W. D. Browne, a young musician of exceptional promise who had been one of his best friends at Rugby. (The fact that so many young friends of Edward Marsh were in the same unit was no coincidence; Marsh was Private Secretary to Churchill.) Browne was killed at Gallipoli a few weeks later. These four buried Brooke on top of a high hill on the island. The long procession was led by a sailor carrying an enormous white cross with Brooke's name written on it in black. The procession took two hours to reach the peak of the hill. The burial took place. The Last Post was sounded, and the grave was marked with slabs of marble that were lying about. The lamp-lit column made the long march down again – and a legend was born. Brooke left his royalties to Lascelles Abercrombie, Wilfrid Gibson and Walter de la Mare, thus providing them with literary independence for the rest of their lives. A naval party landed at Scyros in 1960 and found the grave in an overgrown and dilapidated condition. *Collected Poems* (Sidgwick & Jackson, 1933).

*LESLIE COULSON. Born in 1889. A well-known Fleet Street journalist before the war, he joined the 2nd Royal Fusiliers in September, 1914. He left England in December, 1914, never to return. He went first to Gallipoli where he was wounded; recovered in hospital in Egypt. He was then sent to France, where he was killed in action at the Battle of the Somme, October 7, 1916, aged 27. He was a platoon sergeant at the time of his death. *From an*

Outpost and Other Poems (Erskine Macdonald, 1917) sold 10,000 copies in less than twelve months.

E. E. CUMMINGS. Born in 1894, the son of a Congregational minister, and educated at Harvard. He went to France in the war, and served as an ambulance driver, until interned by the French; wrote a famous war book, *The Enormous Room*. His poetry became well-known for its typographical oddities and ironic-romantic style. He wrote a number of war poems, mostly collected in *Tulips and Chimneys* (1923) and *Collected Poems* (Harcourt, Brace, 1938). He was also a painter. Died in 1962.

*JEFFERY DAY. Born at St Ives, Hunts., 1896, and educated at Repton. An admirer of Rupert Brooke, he joined the Royal Naval Air Service, and became a sub-lieutenant at eighteen. He soon became one of the most famous pilots, credited with legendary exploits. He was shot down by German planes; was awarded the D.S.C. ('for great skill and bravery as a pilot'). He wrote a number of his war poems actually in the air. Aged twenty-one he was promoted to flight-commander. On February 27, 1918, he engaged six enemy aircraft single-handed, and was shot down and killed. *Poems and Rhymes* (Sidgwick & Jackson, 1919). The poem here was first published in *The Cornhill*.

GEOFFREY DEARMER. Born in Lambeth, 1893, and educated at Westminster and Christ Church, Oxford. Fought at Gallipoli, and at the Somme. *Poems* (Heinemann, 1918). Poet, novelist, and playwright. Examiner of Plays to the Lord Chamberlain, 1936–58. Editor, Children's Hour, B.B.C., 1939–59.

de STEIN. See STEIN.

JOHN DRINKWATER. Born in Leytonstone, 1882, the son of a schoolmaster who turned actor. Educated: Oxford High School, Birmingham University. He was an insurance clerk in Birmingham for twelve years, but like his father was attracted to the theatre. Spent much of the war working with (Sir) Barry Jackson at the famous Birmingham Repertory Theatre, as actor, lyricist, and later as stage manager. He died at Kilburn in 1937. *Olton Pools* (Sidgwick & Jackson, 1916). Wrote war play: $x = o$ (1917).

LORD DUNSANY. Born in 1878, and educated at Eton. The 18th Baron. Fought in Boer War. Captain, Royal Inniskilling Fusiliers; Western Front. Wounded in April, 1916. He wrote over 70 books and plays. *Fifty Poems* (G. P. Putnam, 1929). He died in 1957.

J. GRIFFYTH FAIRFAX. Born in Australia, 1886. Educated at Winchester and New College, Oxford. First volume of poetry published in 1908. Called to the Bar, 1912. Captain, R.A.S.C., attached to the 15th Indian Division, 1914–19. Served in Mesopotamia; mentioned in despatches four times. *Mesopotamia* (Murray, 1919). Poet and translator. Member of Parliament (C.) for Norwich, 1924–29.

GILBERT FRANKAU. Born in 1884, and educated at Eton. Travelled around the world before the war. Commissioned in the East Surrey Regiment, 1914. Transferred to Royal Artillery, 1915. Fought at Loos, Ypres, and the Somme. Invalided out with rank of captain, February, 1918. His first poems were published before the war; wrote many war poems. *The City of Fear* (Chatto & Windus, 1917). Also *The Judgement of Valhalla* (Chatto & Windus, 1918). Novelist. Squadron-leader, R.A.F., 1940–41. Died in 1952.

JOHN FREEMAN. Born in 1880, at Dalton, Middlesex, the son of a commercial traveller. He rose rapidly as a business-man, from clerk to director (of the London Victoria Friendly Society). Kept his literary and business associates each in ignorance of his other activity. Became Chief Executive Officer in the Department of National Health and Insurance. His poems at the outbreak of war were possibly the most fervent and deeply felt of all those written at the time. He was awarded the Hawthornden Prize in 1920, and died in 1929. *Collected Poems* (Macmillan, 1928).

CROSBIE GARSTIN. Born in 1887, and educated at private schools and in Germany. A cowboy, lumberjack, etc., in America and Canada, but returned to England on the outbreak of war, and joined 1st King Edward's Horse. Commissioned in the field, 1915. Wrote several popular war poems; this one was first published in *Punch*. Novelist, and writer of the sea, after the war. Died in 1930.

WILFRID GIBSON. Born at Hexham, Northumberland, 1878. A social worker in the East End of London, he was one of Rupert Brooke's closest friends (Brooke called him 'Wibson'). From his very first visit to London he came under the wing of Edward Marsh. Served in the ranks from 1914, but only spent a short time at the Front. He had published several volumes of poetry by the outbreak of war. A prolific poet, he, like Robert Service, celebrated the private soldier. *Collected Poems 1905–25* (Macmillan, 1926). He died in 1962, leaving £10,000.

ROBERT GRAVES. Born in London, 1895, the son of poet and editor A. P. Graves. At Charterhouse and St John's College, Oxford. He served in France with The Royal Welch Fusiliers. A friend of Sassoon, Owen (q.v.), and Nichols. He was reported 'Died of Wounds' on his twenty-first birthday. *Fairies and Fusiliers* (Heinemann, 1917) and *Poems 1914–26* (Heinemann, 1927). After the war he became the Professor of English Literature at Cairo, on the recommendation of T. E. Lawrence and others. *Goodbye to all That*. Historical novelist and poet, he lives much of the time in Majorca. He has disparaged his own war poetry, excluding it nearly all from his collections. Professor of Poetry, Oxford University.

*JULIAN GRENFELL. Born 1888, the eldest son of Lord Desborough. Eton and Balliol, Oxford. He joined the Army as a regular officer in 1910, having passed in first among university graduate entrants. Royal Dragoons; D.S.O.; mentioned in despatches twice. He wrote several poems, but is chiefly remembered for his remarkable 'Into Battle', one of the most anthologized poems of the century. It was first published in *The Times*, 1915, having been sent home in a letter: 'Here is a poem – if you can read it. I rather like it'. A few weeks after completing it he died of wounds, aged 27, on April 30, 1915. His brilliant younger brother Billy, who was about to be elected to All Souls, was killed in action at Hooge two months later. The Desborough title is extinct. *Julian Grenfell*, by Viola Meynell (Burnes, Oates & Washbourne). Grenfell's few poems are uncollected. He wrote in 'Into Battle': 'If this be the last song you shall sing, sing well, for you may not sing another'. It was his last; and he sang well.

WYN GRIFFITH. Born in 1890, and educated at Dolgelly Grammar School. Western Front; commissioned; fought at the Somme. Griffith wrote one of the great war books, *Up to Mametz*. He became Assistant Secretary, Inland Revenue. *The Song Is Theirs* (Penwork, Cardiff, 1947).

THOMAS HARDY. Born at Bockhampton, in Dorset, 1840 – the son of a builder. Started life as an architect, but turned to literature. First novel published in 1871; first volume of poetry, 1898. Made the rural Wessex where he spent much of his life the scene of most of his melancholy novels and much of his poetry. His epic work *The Dynasts* was published between 1903–08. His 'Channel Firing', so strangely prophetic in mood, was written four months before the outbreak of war. *Satires of Circumstance* (1914). *Thomas Hardy* (Penguin, 1960). Died at Dorchester, 1928.

F. W. HARVEY. Born in Gloucestershire in 1888; he wrote much of his poetry about his beloved county. A solicitor, he served in the trenches on the Western Front, but was taken prisoner in 1916. His poems from the prisoner-of-war camps at Crefeld and Gutersloh were mailed to London by the camp authorities. They were immediately published and met with great success; they expressed a natural longing for home, friends and family. *Gloucestershire Friends* (Sidgwick & Jackson, 1917). Also, *Comrades in Captivity.*

A. P. HERBERT. Sir Alan Herbert: born 1890. Educated at Winchester and New College, Oxford. Lieutenant in the Royal Naval Division at Gallipoli, where he was mentioned in despatches, and in France, where he was wounded. Fought at the Somme. He wrote many war verses, some of them published in *Punch*. *The Bomber Gypsy* (Methuen, 2nd edition, revised and enlarged, 1919), and *Half-Hours at Helles* (Blackwell, 1916). He became famous after the war for his writings in *Punch* and work in musical comedy. Member of Parliament (Independent) for Oxford University, 1935–50; knighted in 1945. His daughter married one of the poets of the Second World War, John Pudney.

*W. N. HODGSON. Son of the Bishop of St Edmundsbury and Ipswich, he was born in 1893, and educated at Durham School, where he was an outstanding athlete. An Exhibitioner at Christ Church, he came under the influence of Rupert Brooke. He volunteered on the outbreak of war, and enlisted in the Devonshire Regiment. Served in France; mentioned in despatches; awarded the Military Cross in 1915. Hodgson wrote some prose as well as poetry, including some powerful short stories which showed, perhaps, more promise than his verse. His war poems were published in *The Spectator, Saturday Post*, etc. He was killed on the first day of the Battle of the Somme, July 1, 1916. His *Verse and Prose in Peace and War* (Murray, 1917) quickly ran into three editions.

A. E. HOUSMAN. Born in 1859, the son of a Bromsgrove solicitor. Bromsgrove School, and St John's College, Oxford. Worked in the Patent Office, but his reputation as a classicist was such that when the Professor of Greek and Latin at University College, London, died, he got the Chair on the strength of seventeen testimonials. Later, he was offered the Chair at Cambridge, and, unmarried, he lived there in his rooms at Trinity till his death in 1936. A well-known poet by 1914, on account of his slim volume *A Shropshire Lad. Collected Poems* (Cape, 1939).

PHILIP JOHNSTONE. *High Wood* was first published in *The Nation*, February 16, 1918. It was also published in the anthology *Vain Glory* (Cassell) by Guy Chapman.

DAVID JONES. Born 1895 in Kent. An art student before the war, he served with the 15th Royal Welch Fusiliers, 1915–18, in France and Flanders. His book *In Parenthesis* (Faber, 1937) was one of the most famous of all the 1914–18 war books and one of the last to be published. It received the Hawthornden Prize in 1938. Jones became a leading water-colourist, and his work is exhibited at the Tate Gallery, Victoria and Albert Museum, etc. C.B.E.

*T. M. KETTLE. Born 1880, the son of a famous Irish land reformer. Became in turn a lawyer, a Member of Parliament (N. E. Tyrone, 1906–10), and the Professor of National Economics at University College, Dublin. Poet, journalist, essayist, and idealist. A leading Irish Nationalist, he joined the Dublin Fusiliers when Belgium was attacked, to fight 'not for England, but for small nations'. A friend of the revolutionary and nationalist Pearse, he was one of the outstanding Irishmen of his generation. Wrote a number of war poems, while going through agonies of misery and homesickness in the trenches. Killed in action at the Battle of the Somme, September 8, 1916. *Poems and Parodies* (Duckworth, 1916), and *The Ways of War* (Constable, 1917).

RUDYARD KIPLING. Born in Bombay, 1865. Related to Stanley Baldwin. Educated at United Services College (now Haileybury and I.S.C.); worked for seven years as a journalist. Awarded the Nobel Prize for literature, 1907. His many verses in praise of the ordinary soldier were not fashionable among the young poets of the time, although they were practically the only verse known to the ordinary soldiers themselves. His early poems of the war were suitably stirring, but already contained undertones of doubt and uncertainty as to what it was going to demand. In 1915 his only son, a lieutenant in the Irish Guards, was killed in action at Loos. His war verse became bitter. He devoted much of his time after the war to writing the history of the Irish Guards; one of the finest of regimental histories. He refused the Poet Laureateship on three occasions. *Rudyard Kipling's Verse* (Hodder & Stoughton, 1940). By endowment he contributed for many years to the Last Post being sounded every night at the Menin Gate Memorial, Ypres. He died in 1936.

*FRANCIS LEDWIDGE. Born in Ireland, 1891. He knew Lord Dunsany, who introduced him to Edward Marsh in the hope that Marsh would publish him in the periodical *Georgian Poetry*. Ledwidge wrote nearly all his poetry about Ireland and the fairies. He went to the Western Front with the Royal Irish Fusiliers in 1916, where he continued to write of 'fairy places' and 'the little fields that call across the world to me'. He wrote little of the war. James Stephens wrote of him: 'His promise is, I think, greater than that of any young poet now writing'. Harold Monro had a different view and tried to persuade Edward Marsh to keep him out of *Georgian Poetry* until he was more proficient. Ledwidge was killed in action in Flanders on July 31, 1917. *Last Songs* (Herbert Jenkins, 1918).

P. H. B. LYON. Born in 1893, and educated at Rugby and Oriel College, Oxford. Served in France and Flanders with the 6th Durham Light Infantry; captain. Military Cross, 1917. Wounded, 1918. *Songs of Youth and War* (Erskine Macdonald, 1918). He won the Newdigate Prize with his poem *France* in 1919. Rector of Edinburgh Academy, 1926–31; Headmaster of Rugby, 1931–48. *Now To Be Still and Rest* was first published in *The Spectator*.

D. S. MacCOLL. Born in Glasgow, 1859. Glasgow Academy, University College, London, and Lincoln College, Oxford. Keeper of the Wallace Collection, 1911–24. *Bull and Other War Verses* (Constable, 1919). Died in 1948.

*JOHN McCRAE. Born in 1872. A Canadian doctor, who started to write verse at McGill University. Wrote an important book on pathology. He became well-known as a doctor and socialite. Went to Europe in 1914 as a gunner, but transferred to the Medical Service. *In Flanders Fields* first appeared anonymously in *Punch*, on December 8, 1915. It became the most famous poem of the war. It was written during the second Battle of Ypres. McCrae had his dressing-station during the battle in a hole in the bank of the Ypres Canal, 'into which men literally rolled when shot'. He was put in charge of No. 3 General Hospital at Boulogne. In January, 1918, he was appointed consultant to all the British Armies in France, but died of pneumonia before he could take up the appointment. *In Flanders Fields and Other Poems*, by Lieutenant-Colonel John McCrae, M.D. (Hodder & Stoughton, 1919). Other Canadian war poets were F. G. SCOTT and SMALLEY SARSON.

PATRICK MacGILL. Born Donegal, 1890. *Soldier Songs* (1916).

*E. A. MACKINTOSH. Born in 1893, and educated at St Paul's and Christ Church, Oxford. Left Oxford to join 5th Seaforth Highlanders, and was sent to France where he was awarded the Military Cross. Wounded and gassed at High Wood during the Somme battle. Trained the cadet corps at Cambridge for eight months, during which time he became engaged. He returned to the Front in 1917, and was killed in action at Cambrai in October. *A Highland Regiment* (John Lane, 1917); *War, The Liberator* (1918).

*R. B. MARRIOTT-WATSON. Lieutenant in the Royal Irish Rifles. Killed in action, March 24, 1918. This poem was first published in *The Observer*, 1918.

A. A. MILNE. Born in 1882, and educated at Westminster and Trinity College, Cambridge. Assistant Editor of *Punch*, 1906–14. Commissioned in The Royal Warwickshire Regiment as the result of an introduction to the colonel from A. P. Graves, father of Robert Graves. Fought at what he described as 'the bloodbath of the Somme'. Made battalion Signals Officer. Wrote war verse in *Punch*, which was mostly collected, with others, in *The Sunny Side* (Methuen, 1921). Journalist, novelist, playwright, and children's writer. Died in 1956.

HAROLD MONRO. Born in Brussels, of Scots parents, in 1879. Educated at Radley and Caius College, Cambridge. His first volume of poetry was published in 1906. Author, editor, publisher, and bookseller. He published most of the Georgian poets, and kept bed-sitting-rooms above his bookshop for young poets; Owen, Gibson and T. E. Hulme stayed there. Commissioned in an anti-aircraft battery, R.A. Later posted to the War Office. Wrote several war poems of which the best-known was probably *Youth in Arms*. *Collected Poems* (Cobden-Sanderson, 1933). Died in 1932.

SIR HENRY NEWBOLT. Born in 1862, the son of a Stafford-shire vicar. At Clifton with Douglas Haig. After Oxford (Corpus Christi College) he became a lawyer for twelve years, but gave it up for fulltime writing. Chiefly remembered for *Drake's Drum*, and other songs and verse of the sea. His patriotic verse before the war, with its ideals of duty and obligation to country, is sometimes credited with helping to kindle the prevailing mood of 1914. He was knighted in 1915. After the war he helped to write the official history of the Navy 1914–18. Died in 1938. *St George's Day and Other Poems* (Murray, 1918).

ROBERT NICHOLS. Born in 1893, and educated at Win-chester and Trinity College, Oxford. Served in Royal Artillery, October 1914–August 1916. Fought at the Somme; but soon in-valided home with shellshock. He then went to America with the

British Mission (Ministry of Information). A close friend of Brooke and Sassoon, he was in the Georgian poets group; one of Edward Marsh's most favoured poets. Preceded Edmund Blunden as Professor of English Literature, University of Tokyo, 1921–24. *Invocations* (1915); *Ardours and Endurances* (Chatto & Windus, 1917). He died in 1944.

*WILFRED OWEN. Born at Oswestry, 1893, and educated at Birkenhead Institute and University of London. Worked as a private tutor near Bordeaux, 1913–15, and during this time is reputed to have been influenced by modern French poetry. Despite delicate health, he enlisted in the Artist's Rifles in 1915, and was later commissioned in the Manchester Regt.; served in trenches in France from January, 1917, to June, 1917, when he was invalided home. His nerves shattered, he was sent to the same hospital in Scotland as Sassoon, who discovered the new poet, and who soon afterwards introduced him to Graves and Nichols. After Sassoon's advice and encouragement, Owen became filled with confidence about his own powers. The four poets stayed together on leave in North Wales. Graves's letter to Edward Marsh on this occasion brought first news to London of the new poet: 'I have found a new poet for you, just discovered, one Wilfred Owen: this is a real find, not a sudden lo here! or lo there! . . . but the real thing, when we've educated him a trifle more. R.N. and S.S. and myself are doing it' (from Christopher Hassall, op. cit.). Blunden wrote 'the impact of Sassoon's character, thought, and independent poetic method gave Owen a new purpose'. Shortly before returning to France, Owen wrote in a letter to Osbert Sitwell (also introduced to him by Sassoon) in July, 1918: 'For fourteen hours yesterday I was at work – teaching Christ to lift his cross by numbers, and how to adjust his crown; . . . I attended his supper to see that there were no complaints; and inspected the feet to see that they should be worthy of the nails . . . with maps I made him familiar with the topography of Golgotha' (from *Pleasures of New Writing*, Lehmann, 1952). Owen returned to the same battalion at the Front, and was

Company Commander. He wrote to his mother: 'I came out in order to help these boys; directly, by leading them as well as an officer can; indirectly, by watching their sufferings that I may speak of them as well as a pleader can.' Towards the end, he wrote: 'My senses are charred; I don't take the cigarette out of my mouth when I write Deceased over their letters.' In October, he was awarded the Military Cross for exceptional bravery in the field. He was killed by machine-gun fire on November 4, 1918, while endeavouring to get his company across the Sambre Canal. By most critics he is considered to be the outstanding poet of the war. His use of the half-rhyme was well-suited to his sombre subject and mood; it was widely copied by poets in the inter-war years. Sir Osbert Sitwell has written of 'Strange Meeting': 'as great a poem as exists in our tongue'. John Wain has written: 'Is there a finer war poem in world literature than 'Anthem For Doomed Youth'?' *Poems* with an Introduction by Siegfried Sassoon (Chatto & Windus, 1920); *Collected Poems* with an Introduction by Edmund Blunden (Chatto & Windus, 1931); *Collected Poems*, edited by C. Day Lewis (Chatto & Windus, 1963); *Wilfred Owen: A Critical Study* by D. S. R. Welland (Chatto & Windus, 1960); *Journey From Obscurity* by Harold Owen (Oxford, 1963).

*NOWELL OXLAND. This poem, written on the way to Gallipoli, while Oxland was serving with the 6th Border Regiment, was first published in *The Times*, 1915. Oxland was killed in action at Suvla Bay, August 9, 1915.

*ROBERT PALMER. Lord Selborne writes of his brother: 'Robert Stafford Arthur Palmer was the second son of the second Earl of Selborne, and was born in 1888. Educated at Winchester, where he became head of the school, he gained a scholarship at University College, Oxford, a first in Honour Mods. and in Greats. Deeply religious, he was President of the Union, and the University Church Union. He was called to the Bar in 1913, where he worked as a pupil under Mr Rayner Goddard (Lord Goddard) who pro-

phesied that he would be one of the foremost lawyers of his genera-
tion, and later said that he would undoubtedly have become Lord
Chancellor if he had lived. At the outbreak of War, in August,
1914, he joined the 6th Battalion, Royal Hampshire Regiment, and
was killed at the Battle of Umm-Al-Hannal, in Mesopotamia,
January 21, 1916.' Palmer was the grandson of Lord Salisbury, and
a cousin of Viscount Grey of Falloden; his godfather was Arthur
Balfour. Knew A. P. Herbert and Julian Grenfell. He travelled
widely before the war, wrote some poetry, a book on India, and
political pamphlets. He was offered the Dean and Fellowship in
Divinity at New College, Oxford. *The Life of Robert Palmer* by
Laura Ridding (Hodder & Stoughton, 1921). This poem, sent home
n a letter, was first published in *The Times*, October 15, 1915.

MAX PLOWMAN. Born at Tottenham, 1883. Commissioned in
the 10th West Yorks. Regt.; fought at the Somme. The collection
A Lap Full of Seed (Blackwell) appeared in 1917. He later wrote one
of the most moving war books, *A Subaltern on the Somme*, under
the pseudonym of Mark VII, and four books of verse. His war
experiences turned him towards pacifism. Secretary of the Peace
Pledge Union, 1937–38. Editor of *The Adelphi*, 1938–41. Died in
1941.

HERBERT READ. Born in Yorkshire, 1893, the son of a
brewer. Educated at Leeds University. Served with the Green
Howards, 1915–18. Captain, 1917. Western Front; Military Cross,
D.S.O., mentioned in despatches. After the war he became a Civil
Servant, before taking up an academic and literary career as pro-
fessor and lecturer in fine arts and poetry. He was knighted in 1953.
Naked Warriors (1919); *Collected Poems* (Faber, 1946); *The Contrary
Experience* (Faber, 1963).

EDGELL RICKWORD. Born in 1898. A friend of W. J
Turner, he fought on the Western Front, and his war poems were
published in many periodicals at the time. After the war, poet and
biographer. *Behind The Eyes* (Sidgwick & Jackson, 1921);

Invocation to Angels (Wishart, 1928); *Collected Poems* (Bodley Head, 1947).

*ISAAC ROSENBERG. Born in Bristol, 1890; but his family moved to the East End of London when he was still a child. Educated at the Stepney Board School, where his gifts for drawing and writing were so remarkable that he was allowed to devote all his time to them. He left school at fourteen, but he had already written his first poems – at the age of twelve. He took up art, and friends provided the means to send him to the Slade School for two and a half years. He exhibited at the Whitechapel Gallery. Rosenberg was first encouraged in his poetry by Laurence Binyon, to whom he wrote, and then by Marsh, who took him under his capacious wing. He went on a trip to South Africa, to try to improve his suspect lungs. He enlisted in the King's Own Royal Lancaster Regiment in 1915, partly in the hope that his mother would benefit from the separation allowance. No one could have been less-fitted for military service. As well as having weak lungs, Rosenberg was extremely short; he was also acutely absent-minded, which caused him many fatigues and punishments. He fought in the trenches on the Western Front, and was killed in action on April 1, 1918. Some critics consider him the best of the war poets after Wilfred Owen. *Collected Poems* (Heinemann, 1922).

SIEGFRIED SASSOON. Born in 1886, and educated at Marlborough and Clare College, Cambridge. His early idyllic life of hunting, cricket and country pursuits was disturbed by the war. He served with the Sussex Yeomanry, and then with the Royal Welch Fusiliers (in a different battalion to his close friend of the time, Robert Graves). By all accounts an officer of exceptional courage, he was known as 'Kangers' and 'Mad Jack'. Won the Military Cross just before the Battle of the Somme. Later was in hospital at Craiglockhart with his admirer Wilfred Owen (q.v.), who wrote of him: 'I hold you as Keats + Christ + Elijah + my Colonel + my father confessor + Amenophis IV in profile'. He was the first to write sustained poetry critical of the progress of the war; he described its horrors unsparingly. By the end of the war acknowledged leader and hero of all the younger poets. After the war he was Literary Editor of the *Daily Herald*, and started on his great autobiography. The first part, *Memoirs of a Fox-Hunting Man*, gained both the Hawthornden and James Tait Black Memorial Prizes. The second part, *Memoirs of an Infantry Officer*, were unsurpassed as memoirs of the war. C.B.E., 1951. Lives in Wiltshire. *The War Poems of Siegfried Sassoon* (Heinemann, 1919); *Collected Poems 1908–56* (Faber, 1961).

R. H. SAUTER. *Songs in Captivity* (Heinemann, 1922), by the nephew of Galsworthy.

*ALAN SEEGER. Born 1888, in New York. He lived in Mexico as a child, then went to Harvard. He went to live in Paris in 1912, where he led the traditional bohemian life. He went to London in the summer of 1914, and researched in the British Museum Library. After three weeks of war he joined the French Foreign Legion with a group of forty Americans. Almost immediately his poetry, which previously had been unsuccessful, began to be published. He became a kind of vigorous, American Rupert Brooke. Fought at Champagne (where he was reported killed) and at the Somme. Mowed down and killed with nearly all his comrades at the Somme on July 4, 1916, when six German machine-guns caught them in enfilade fire. His death was widely reported in the American newspapers, and he became a minor legend. *Poems* (Constable, 1917 – in the United States: Charles Scribner).

ROBERT SERVICE. Born in Preston, 1874. Went to Canada, where he wrote novels, and a vast quantity of down-to-earth verse. He became a stretcher-bearer (in his forties) during the war, and served on the Western Front in France and Flanders. Wrote many poems of 'the poor bloody infantry'. *Collected Verse* (Benn, 1930).

EDWARD SHANKS. Born in 1892, and educated at Merchant Taylor's and Trinity College, Cambridge. Had an uneasy relationship with the Georgian poets of Edward Marsh and Harold Monro. Joined the 8th South Lancashire Regiment in 1914, but invalided out the following year. Worked in the War Office for the remainder of the war. First winner of the Hawthornden Prize, in 1919. Lecturer in Poetry, University of Liverpool, 1926. Chief leader-writer of the *Evening Standard*, 1928–35. *Poems 1912–32* (Macmillan, 1933). Died in 1953.

*PATRICK SHAW-STEWART. Born 1888, the son of a major-general, and educated at Eton and Balliol College, Oxford, with Julian Grenfell. One of Edward Marsh's most favoured young friends. Rupert Brooke described him as 'the most brilliant man they've had in Oxford for ten years'. Hertford and Ireland Scholarships; Double First. Lieutenant-commander, Naval Div. With Brooke at his death. Fought at Gallipoli, where he wrote in a letter home: 'I continue to believe that the luck of my generation must change . . . nowadays we who are alive have the sense of being old, old survivors.' Killed in action in France, 1917, having refused to go back after his ear had been torn off by shrapnel a few minutes before. A biography of him was written by Ronald Knox: *Patrick Shaw-Stewart* (Collins, 1920).

OSBERT SITWELL. Baronet. Born in 1892, and educated at Eton ('during the holidays'). He joined the Grenadier Guards in 1912. His book *Great Morning* gives an account of the sad state of affairs in the British army on the eve of the war. Fought at Loos. Served with E. W. Tennant (q.v.). He helped his sister Edith edit *Wheels*, a rival publication to the *Georgian Poetry* of Marsh and Monro; several of the war poets first appeared in it. His war poetry became increasingly bitter; a poem in celebration of the Armistice was entitled *Corpse Day*. Friendly with Sassoon and Owen (q.v.), whose feelings he shared. *Selected Poems Old and New* (Duckworth,

1943); *Argonaut and Juggernaut* (Chatto & Windus, 1919). Writer of short stories, novels, and autobiography; engaged in 'a series of skirmishes and hand-to-hand battles against the philistine'.

*C. H. SORLEY. Born in Aberdeen, 1895, and educated at Marlborough. He won a scholarship to University College, Oxford, but enlisted in the Suffolk Regiment in August, 1914. He was soon in the trenches, and by the following August held the rank of captain. He was killed in action, aged 20, at Loos on October 13, 1915. His *Marlborough and Other Poems* (Cambridge University Press, 1916) quickly ran into four editions. His *Song of The Ungirt Runners* has been widely anthologized, and learnt by many a schoolboy. Sorley had an extraordinarily well-developed gift for rhyming. John Masefield considered him the most promising of the war poets. Sorley wrote in a letter home, enclosing some poems: 'You will notice that most of what I have written is as hurried and angular as the handwriting: written out at different times and dirty with my pocket: but I have had no time for the final touch nor seem likely to have for some time.'

EDWARD DE STEIN. Born in 1887, and educated at Eton and Magdalen College, Oxford. K.R.R.C., 1914–18; Western Front; attained rank of major. Wrote about twenty published war poems, mostly in *The Times, Bystander, Punch*, etc., about the fellowship of the trenches and 'that perpetual sense of the ridiculous which, even under the most appalling conditions, never seemed to desert the men with whom I was privileged to serve, and which indeed seemed to flourish more freely in the mud and rain of the front line than in the comparative comfort of billets.' *The Poets in Picardy and Other Poems* (Murray, 1919) is his only publication. Knighted in 1946. President of Gallaher's Tobacco.

*E. W. TENNANT. Hon. Edward Wyndham Tennant, born 1897, the son of Lord Glenconner. He was educated at Winchester, but left school at seventeen to join the Grenadier Guards

(4th Battalion) – the youngest Wykehamist to enlist. He was an extremely popular, but sensitive young man, devoted to his mother, who was also a writer. He was specially selected to go to France (despite a Brigade order that no one under nineteen should be sent). He served a year in the trenches. For a time he was in the same company as Osbert Sitwell – they shared a dug-out. His poems started appearing in magazines and periodicals while he was at the Front. He was killed in action at the Battle of the Somme (which had begun on his nineteenth birthday), September 22, 1916. He was buried beside his friend Raymond Asquith. *Worple Flit and Other Poems* (Blackwell, 1916), and *Hon. E. W. Tennant*, by Pamela Glenconner (John Lane, 1919); the latter book, by his mother, who later married Viscount Grey of Falloden, contains the remainder of his poetry. 'The Mad Soldier' first appeared in Edith Sitwell's collection *Wheels* (second edition), and 'Home Thoughts in Laventie' in *The Times*, 1916.

*EDWARD THOMAS. Born in 1878; educated at St Paul's School, and Lincoln College, Oxford. He was encouraged to write poetry by his friend Robert Frost, who was living at the time in England, and he became a member of the Georgian group of poets. Worked for the *Daily Chronicle*. His friends included Lascelles Abercrombie and Rupert Brooke. Joined the Artist's Rifles, and was soon in the trenches; transferred to the Royal Garrison Artillery. He continued to write his favourite poems of nature and the countryside, even when in the front line, and he wrote few war poems. He was killed in action at Arras, April 9, 1917. *Collected Poems* (Ingpen & Grant, 1922); *Edward Thomas: The Last Four Years* (Oxford, 1958) by Eleanor Farjeon.

EDWARD THOMPSON. Born at Stockport in 1886. Worked in a bank at Bethnal Green, before studying at London University, and being ordained as a Wesleyan minister. A minister in India before the war, he was appointed Chaplain to the 7th Division,

Mesopotamia, in 1916. Wrote a number of war poems from 'Mespot'. Resigned his ministry in India in 1923 to live as a scholar and poet in Oxford. *Collected Poems* (Benn, 1930). Died: 1946. His son Frank, killed in 1944, was a World War II poet.

W. J. TURNER. Born in Melbourne, Australia, 1889. Travelled in South Africa and Europe till the outbreak of war. He met Rupert Brooke and the Georgian poets in London. Served in the Royal Artillery, 1916-18. Succeeded Sassoon as Literary Editor of the *Daily Herald*. Novelist, essayist, and poet. *Selected Poems*, 1916-36 (Oxford University Press, 1939). He died in 1946.

*R. E. VERNÈDE. Born in London, 1875. Educated at St Paul's School, and St John's College, Oxford. A friend of G. K. Chesterton, whom he first met at school. Wrote several novels before the war. Enlisted in 9th Royal Fusiliers, September, 1914. Went to France, attached to the 3rd Rifle Brigade. Wounded at the Somme in 1916, but insisted on returning to the Front after leaving hospital in England, although he was offered a job in the War Office. Killed in action by machine-gun fire, April 9, 1917, leading his platoon in an attack on Havrincourt Wood: aged 41. He left a widow. *War Poems*, with an Introduction by Edmund Gosse (Heinemann, 1918).

ALEC WAUGH. Born in Hampstead, 1898, the son of a publisher; brother of Evelyn Waugh. Educated at Sherborne, and Sandhurst. The Dorset Regiment, 1917-18. He wrote some particularly bitter war verse, such as 'Cannon Fodder', towards the end of the war. A prisoner-of-war, 1918. He received reviews of *The Loom of Youth* (1917), a sensational novel about his schooldays, while fighting at Passchendaele. *Resentment* (Grant Richards, 1918). Author.

WILLOUGHBY WEAVING. Educated at Pembroke College, Oxford, he was a protégé of Robert Bridges. An Irishman, he served as a lieutenant in The Royal Irish Fusiliers on the Western Front. He was a prolific poet of the Irish and English country-side, and his poetry about nature achieved wide popularity. Invalided home: 1915. *The Star Fields and Other Poems* (Blackwell, 1916).

I. A. WILLIAMS. Born in Middlesborough, 1890, the son of an M.P. Educated at Rugby, and King's College, Cambridge. He served in France and Flanders, 1914-18, attaining the rank of captain. His first volume of *Poems* (Macmillan) was published in 1915; also *New Poems* (Methuen, 1919). Worked on the *London Mercury* and *The Times*. Bibliographer.

*T. P. CAMERON WILSON. A young, unknown school-master, he joined the Sherwood Foresters, and quickly rose to the rank of captain. He was killed in action in the Somme valley, March 23, 1918. *Magpies in Picardy*, and other war verse, was pub-lished by Harold Monro and *The Poetry Bookshop*. It attracted little attention but was rescued by Field Marshal Lord Wavell from the oblivion of many years when he included it in his war-time anthology *Other Men's Flowers* (Cape, 1944). The version of *Magpies in Picardy* that appeared in Monro's collection omitted the last two verses. But Wavell, with his extraordinary memory, had remembered them from the time they first appeared in the *West-minster Gazette*. (*Wavell: Portrait of a Soldier*, by Bernard Fergusson, Collins, 1961.)

W. B. YEATS. Born in 1865, and educated in Hammersmith and Dublin. He spent most of the war between his London rooms, Lady Gregory's house near Galway, and, after his marriage in 1917 at the age of 52, in Oxford. The Easter Rising of 1916, in Dublin, moved him more than did the Western Front. He had little sym-pathy with the war poets, from whom he mostly remained aloof (q.v. Introductory Note), but he had sufficient vision of the

experience of his countrymen to write one great war poem included
here. Died in the South of France, 1939. His remains were brought
back to Ireland in 1948 by the Irish navy, which thus ventured
outside territorial waters for the first time. *Collected Poems* (Mac-
millan, 1952).

E. HILTON YOUNG. Born in 1879, and educated at Eton,
and Trinity College, Cambridge. Called to the Bar, 1904. R.N.V.R.,
1914. Served at Zeebrugge and Archangel; D.S.O. and D.S.C.
Wounded in 1918. Married the widow of Captain Robert Falcon
Scott. *A Muse at Sea* (Sidgwick & Jackson, 1919). Member of
Parliament, 1915–35. Minister of Health, 1931–35. Became Lord
Kennet. Another volume of verse was published in 1935. He died
in 1960.

FRANCIS BRETT YOUNG. Born in Worcestershire, 1884,
and educated at Epsom College and Birmingham University. Wrote
a critical study of Robert Bridges in 1913. A doctor, he served with
the R.A.M.C. in the rigorous and hungry East African campaign,
with the rank of major. Eventually invalided home with fever and
exhaustion. *Poems 1916–18* (Collins, 1919). Later became a close
friend of Marsh. Poet and novelist. He died in 1954.

INDEX

page references to poems are shown in italic